22x|11-07/2-11

22x(11/07) 1/10

The
Budgie

An Owner's Guide To

A HAPPY HEALTHY PET

Howell Book House

Howell Book House
A Simon & Schuster Macmillan Company
1633 Broadway
New York, NY 10019

Library of Congress Cataloging-in-Publication Data
Rach, Julie.
The budgie: an owner's guide to a happy, healthy pet / Julie Rach.
p. cm.

ISBN 0-87605-500-5

1. Budgerigar.   I. Title.
SF473.B8R25   1997
636.6′864—dc21   96-43525
                      CIP

Manufactured in the United States of America
10 9 8 7 6 5 4 3 2 1

Series Director: Ariel Cannon
Series Assistant Director: Jennifer Liberts
Book Design: Michele Laseau
Cover Design: Iris Jeromnimon
Illustration: Casey Price
Photography:
  Front cover photos: Joan Balzarini
  Back cover photo: B. Everett Webb
  Joan Balzarini: 59
  Scott McKiernan/Zuma Press: 37, 117
  Cheryl Primeau: 10
  Renee Stockdale: 8, 13, 14, 23, 29, 30, 33, 34, 42, 43, 44, 45, 47, 48, 49, 50, 51, 54,
  56, 60, 61, 63, 66, 68, 73, 75, 76, 80, 102, 103, 108, 110, 111, 114
  Faith Uridel: 9
  B. Everett Webb: 2-3, 5, 6, 11, 12, 15, 17, 20, 22, 24, 26-7, 28, 31, 38, 53, 58, 95, 104,
  106, 119, 120, 121, 124
Production Team: Kathleen Caulfield, Trudy Coler, Natalie Hollifield,
  Stephanie Mohler and John Carroll

Contents

Welcome

to the

World

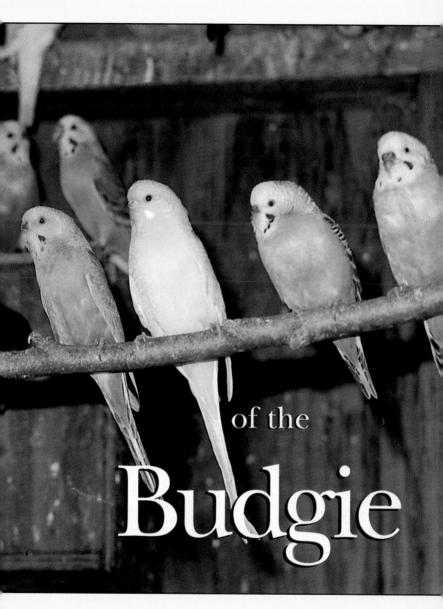

of the

Budgie

External Features of the Budgie

Crown

Nare

Cere

Nape

Mantel

Beak

Rump

Breast

Tail Features
(retrices)

chapter 1

The
Budgie's
Ancestry

Presently, scientists have identified about 750 parrot species. Of these, some 280 are kept as pets, and about 250 of those have bred successfully in captivity, assuring that parrots will be around for future generations to enjoy. Prospective bird owners will find themselves in good company historically, since birds have been kept as pets for centuries.

Birdkeeping Through the Ages

The ancient Egyptians are credited with being the first to keep birds, most notably pigeons. Queen Hatsheput (1504 to 1482 B.C.) was credited as being the first monarch to create a royal zoo, which included exotic birds. The ancient Persians also knew about talking birds as early as the fifth century B.C., when a court physician and naturalist wrote about talking birds described to him by Indian merchants.

CLASSICAL GREECE AND ROME

Cultures around the world have been keeping beautiful birds like this budgie for centuries.

From Egypt, birdkeeping spread to Greece and Rome. Alexander the Great receives credit from some historians with discovering the Alexandrine parakeet, and the Greeks are credited with popularizing parrot-keeping outside of the birds' native lands of Africa and Asia. Pliny the Elder offered instructions in parrot training in the first century A.D., suggesting that each bird should be housed in its own enclosure in a dark room to help it learn to speak more quickly.

Well-to-do Romans built extensive garden aviaries, and they also employed mockingbirds in the entryways of their homes as feathered doorbells to announce visitors. The Romans are thought to have been the first bird dealers, bringing different types of birds to Great Britain and the European continent.

EUROPE

Until the Renaissance, birdkeeping was a hobby that only the wealthy could pursue. After canaries were introduced to Europe by Portuguese sailors, birdkeeping began to take off as a hobby, although it was still confined largely to upper-class fanciers. (Some credit Christopher Columbus with bringing Queen Isabella a pair of Cuban Amazons from the New World and introducing Amazon parrots to European bird fanciers.) In the 1600s, the Dutch began producing varieties of canaries for show. These birds were exported to Britain, and birdkeeping began to be more accessible to the masses.

At about the same time, in the British penal colony of Australia, a forger named Thomas Watling first described the budgerigar's ability to mimic human speech. This bird was able to greet Watling's employer by saying "How do you do, Dr. White?"

Birdkeeping as we know it today can be traced to its beginnings in Victorian Great Britain, when bird sellers in the British Isles would offer goldfinches and larks to ship captains en route to the West Indies. These common European birds would then be traded in the islands for species found there.

Some notable bird owners of history include King Henry VIII, whose African Grey was alleged to have called for help when it fell in the Thames River; Marie Antoinette, who also had an African Grey parrot; Wolfgang Amadeus Mozart, who kept canaries and a pet starling; Thomas Jefferson, who made a pet of a mockingbird; Andrew Jackson, whose parrot, Polly, made life interesting at the White House; and Theodore Roosevelt, whose family kept a Hyacinth Macaw during its stay in the White House.

> **PARROT TRAITS**
>
> The budgie is a species of parrot, just like the Hyacinth Macaw or Mealy Amazon. The traits that all parrot species have in common are
>
> - four toes—two pointing backward and two pointing forward
> - upper beak overhanging the lower
> - broad head and short neck
>
> However, a healthy budgie measures about seven inches from tip of the head to tip of the tail, while a full-grown Scarlet Macaw can easily reach forty inches in length.

The Budgie's Background

Now that we've looked at the history of birdkeeping, let's look at the background of your chosen bird, the budgerigar. Some of you may know budgerigars by their common nickname, budgies. Others may call them parakeets. Both are correct, since the term parakeet generally describes any long-tailed parrot.

TRUE AUSTRALIANS

Budgies come from Australia, where they live in large communal flocks. (These large flocks make budgies naturally sociable birds. If you keep a single pet bird, make sure you fulfill its need for companionship by spending time with it each day.) Many wild budgerigars are found in central Australia, which is a harsh, arid land. To cope with these extreme conditions, budgies have adapted to surviving on minimal food and water requirements. (Notice that I say surviving, and not thriving. Budgerigars kept in captivity need more than seeds and water to thrive.)

The budgie's name is said to come from an Aboriginal phrase that means "good to eat," although I can't imagine eating such personable little birds. The species' scientific name, *Melopsittacus undulatus*, literally means "song parrot with wavy lines," which refers to the birds' melodic voices and the wavy bars across their backs and wings. These wavy lines help wild budgies camouflage themselves in the Australian grasslands so they are less obvious to predators. In the past, budgies were also called shell parrots, warbling grass parakeets and zebra parrots.

One reason for budgies' quick rise to popularity in Europe was their ability to breed easily in captivity.

THE BUDGIE ARRIVES IN EUROPE

The British naturalist John Gould is credited with bringing the budgerigar to the attention of the pet-loving public. In 1838, Gould and his wife, Elizabeth, traveled from London to Australia to study the continent's native wildlife for a series of books Gould was writing. Although he considered budgies rather dull in personality, Gould brought a pair back to England.

Budgies soon became popular pets with upper-class Europeans, and hundreds of thousands of them were sent on weeklong sea voyages from Australia to England, Belgium and Holland. Although many birds died in transit, those that survived proved to be surprisingly easy to breed in captivity (Gould's brother-in-law, Charles Coxen, bred the first pair in England in the 1840s), and they were soon being bred across Europe by zoological gardens and aristocratic birdkeepers. One of the first pair bred by Gould's brother-in-law was sold by a British bird dealer for 27£ sterling, which would be equivalent to several hundred dollars today.

The Antwerp Zoo in Belgium was one of the first places budgies were put on display. Budgie breeding began in earnest in Antwerp in the 1850s, and it soon spread across Europe. France imported 100,000 pairs of birds, and breeding farms were set up in France and Belgium by the end of the 19th century.

Birds were still being exported by the thousands from Australia to Europe, South Africa, South America and the United States. Australia finally banned export of budgerigars in 1894, a ban that is still in place.

The wavy lines on the budgie's back and wings help to camouflage it in the wild.

BUDGIES IN AMERICA

Although they have been kept as pets in America for years, budgies began their current reign of popularity in the United States in the 1950s. Today, about 16 million pet birds are kept in American homes, and 45 percent of them are budgies, according to statistics from the American Pet Product Manufacturers Association. They are the most popularly kept pet parrot in the world, with some 5 million pet and show birds in Great Britain alone.

English and American Budgies

In your search for the perfect pet budgerigar, you may have noticed that there are two types of budgies: the English and the American. The differences between the two birds are slight but noticeable. Budgie breeder Penny Corbett, in her "Ask the Experts" column in *Bird Talk*, describes the differences as follows: "English budgie breeders concentrate their efforts toward breeding a larger, more majestic bird. Budgie competition is much more widespread in England than it is in the United States. Exhibitors in England have spent more time breeding exhibition budgies, and some believe this is how exhibition (or English) budgies got their name."

Today, budgies' small size and gentle nature have made them the most popular pet parrot in the world.

"American budgies are generally regarded as pet birds," Corbett continues. "They are more active than the mellow English birds, and are often bred in large quantities to supply the demand of the pet trade. The American budgie is generally more outgoing, active and mischievous than its counterpart."

Now that we've looked briefly at the budgie's history, let's see why this small parrot has become such a popular pet.

So Why is the Budgie so Popular?

Some of the reasons bird lovers are attracted to budgerigars include their manageable size, their gentleness, their nondestructiveness, the ease with which they can be handled and tamed, their sociable nature and their talking ability, although the last shouldn't be the sole reason for choosing a budgie or any other pet bird.

English budgies tend to be larger and less excitable than their American counterparts. Pictured here are two male English budgies.

A budgie's size makes it an easily handled pet for bird lovers, young or old. A healthy budgie measures about seven inches from the top of its head to the tip of its tail, and it weighs about thirty grams (1.05 ounces). This small size comes with a quiet, pleasant voice and a manageable beak. Since noise and the potential for painful bites deter some would-be bird owners, the budgie offers a welcome alternative from ear-splitting shrieks or serious wounds from bites.

Because budgies have been kept as pets for so many years, some people consider them one of the few domesticated pet birds. They seem to enjoy people and being part of an active family. They also seem to want to please their owners by learning tricks or learning to talk, although I can't guarantee that your budgie will be a trickster or a talker. People choose a budgie as a pet because they want to share their homes with a bird and appreciate it for the unique being that it is.

chapter 2

Choosing
the Right Budgie
for YOU

Before you decide to bring a budgie into your life, you'll need to consider a few questions first. Do you like animals? Do you have time to care for one properly? Can you have pets where you live? Can you live with a little mess (seed hulls, feathers and discarded food) in your home? Can you tolerate, and appreciate, a little noise (the amount made by one exuberant budgie) as part of your daily routine?

Why a Bird?

If you've answered "yes" to all these, you're a good candidate for bird ownership. Now your next question might be "Why do I want a bird?" Here are some of the answers you might come up with:

Birds are relatively quiet pets. Unless you have a particularly vocal macaw or cockatoo, most birds aren't likely to annoy the neighbors the way a barking dog or a yowling cat can. In many rental situations, birds aren't even considered pets, which means you can keep them without having to surrender a sizable security deposit to your landlord.

Amusing and friendly interaction is one of the many reasons people choose a budgie for a pet.

Birds' small size makes them good pets for today's smaller living spaces. More of us are living in apartments, mobile or manufactured homes and condominiums, which makes the ownership of large pets that need yards and lots of regular exercise awkward and inconvenient. Birds just seem to fit better in apartments, condos, mobile homes and other smaller living spaces.

Birds may be easier to maintain than dogs and cats. As one who has had all three types of pets, I think the daily maintenance time a bird requires may be less than what a dog or cat needs. Birds don't have to be walked; they don't require as much grooming as a longhaired dog or cat nor do they shed as much. And there's only a cage and small bowls to clean, instead of bowls and a litter box for a cat or the whole yard in the case of a dog.

Birds interact well with their owners. Although a bird isn't as blindly loyal as the average dog, it isn't as aloof as many cats I've known, either. As an added bonus, many birds can learn to whistle or talk, which is beyond

13

the range of canine and feline ability and which many owners find amusing or entertaining.

Birds are long-lived pets. A cockatoo named King Tut greeted visitors at the San Diego Zoo for 70 years, and *Bird Talk* magazine reported on a documented 106-year-old Amazon in Alaska. Many bird owners I know have made provisions for their larger parrots in their wills. Smaller birds can live long lives, too; the *Guinness Book of Records* reports an almost 30-year-old budgerigar in Great Britain.

Birds require consistent, but not constant, attention. This can be a plus for today's busy single people and families. While birds can't be ignored completely, they are content to entertain themselves for part of the day while their owners are busy elsewhere.

Budgies may be good pets for people who have limited space to house a pet.

I can't tell you how many of my evenings have been brightened with the presence of my bird, Sindbad. He is content to sit on my lap and have his back rubbed or his head scratched while we watch TV together. He asks for very little except regular feedings and cage cleanings and a bit of attention each day, and he offers companionship and unconditional love in return.

Birds provide "a reason to get up in the morning." This cannot be overestimated for older bird owners and single people who are on their own. Birds provide all the benefits realized in the human/animal bond, such as lower blood pressure and reduced levels of stress in owners who interact regularly with their pets.

Finally, **birds are intelligent pets.** Whoever coined the phrase "birdbrain" didn't truly appreciate how smart some birds are. Some larger parrots have scored at levels comparable to chimpanzees, dolphins and pre-school age children on intelligence tests.

Are you purchasing a parakeet on a whim because you're attracted to its bright colors? Are you rescuing a bird from its aggressive cagemates? Are you buying a bird you otherwise feel sorry for? Noble though some of these reasons are, none of them is a good reason for purchasing a pet bird. Birds purchased for their pretty colors may soon be ignored or neglected by owners whose attentions have been captured by another fancy, and small, timid birds may be hiding signs of illness that can be difficult and costly to cure and that can cause an owner much heartache in the process.

If you feel the urge to become a bird owner, and you've bought this book instead, you're on the right road. If you purchased this book along with your parakeet, this is also a good first step, or if you've picked up this book after having your bird a few weeks or months, congratulations! You're on the road to responsible bird ownership.

Budgies and Children

If you plan to purchase a budgie as a child's pet, please keep the following in mind. Children in the primary grades may need some

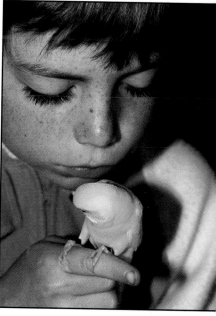

Children who know how to properly handle birds can be great friends with a pet budgie.

help from their parents or from older siblings in caring for their new pet. Children in the intermediate grades should be ready for the responsibility of bird ownership with limited parental supervision. Or the bird can just be "a family pet" with each family member being responsible for some aspect of the bird's care. Even the youngest family members can help out by selecting healthful foods for the bird on a trip to the market or picking out a safe, colorful toy at the bird store.

Parents need to remind children of the following when they're around birds:

1. Approach the cage quietly. Birds don't like to be surprised.

2. Talk softly to the bird. Don't scream or yell at it.

3. Don't shake or hit the cage.

4. Don't poke at the bird or its cage with your fingers, sticks, pencils or other items.

5. If you're allowed to take the bird out of its cage, handle it gently.

6. Don't take the bird outside. In unfamiliar surroundings (such as the outdoors), birds can become confused and fly away from their owners. Most are never recovered.

7. Respect the bird's need for quiet time.

I'd like to remind adults to please not give any live pet as a holiday present. Birthdays, Christmas, Hanukkah and other holidays are exciting but stressful times for both people and animals. A pet coming to a new home is under enough stress just by joining its new family; don't add to its stress by bringing it home for a holiday. Instead, give the child pet-care accessories for the actual celebration and a gift certificate that will allow the child to select his or her pet (with proper parental permission, of course) after the excitement of the special day has died down.

The Bottom Line

Some things you'll want to think about as you become a budgie owner are:

- the cost of the bird itself

- the cost of its cage and accessories

- the cost of bird food (seeds, formulated diets and fresh foods)

- the cost of toys

- the cost of veterinary care
- the amount of time you can devote to your bird each day
- how busy your life is already
- who will care for the bird if you go on vacation or are called out of town unexpectedly
- how many other pets you already own
- the size of your home

If, after considering all these factors, you're still interested in adding a budgie to your home because you want a cheerful companion bird, please read on to learn more about bringing a budgie into your life.

One thing you'll need to consider before bringing a budgie into the family is cost, not only of the bird but of the necessary equipment and veterinary attention.

Where Will You Get Your Budgie?

Budgies can be purchased through several sources, including classified newspaper advertisements, bird shows and marts and pet stores. Let's look at each in a bit more detail.

CLASSIFIED ADVERTISEMENTS

Classified ads are usually placed by private parties who want to place pets in new homes. If the advertiser offers young birds, it is likely to be a private breeder who wants to place a few birds in good homes.

Most pet budgies can leave the breeder's home at around six weeks of age, and the time between six weeks and three months of age is considered by some to be the optimal time to teach a pet budgie to talk and to do tricks. You can tell baby budgies by the series of stripes that cover their heads and necks (the stripes remain on the backs of the birds' necks following the first molt). Young birds also have small, slightly elongated spots on their face masks, while adults have large, round spots, and youngsters also have large, dark eyes that give them particularly endearing looks, where adult birds have well-developed white irises. Baby budgies may also have dark or slightly black beaks.

Some breeders may also offer older birds for sale from time to time. These are most likely breeder birds that are too old to produce chicks but that are still good candidates for pet situations.

If you buy your bird from a private breeder, you will probably be shown only the birds that the breeder has for sale. Do not be offended or upset if you cannot see all the birds that the breeder keeps; some birds are more sensitive than others about the presence of strangers during breeding season, and the sensitive ones may destroy eggs or kill chicks when they're upset. Budgies are less prone to this sensitivity than larger parrots, but a breeder may keep all of his or her nesting pairs in the same area. If, however,

---

BUDGIE OWNER'S SHOPPING LIST

When you go to the pet supply store to pick out your bird's accessories, take a copy of this list along so you won't forget any of the important items your new pet will need to feel right at home!

- a cage

- open food and water bowls (at least two sets of each for easier dish changing and cage cleaning)

- perches of varying diameters and materials

- a sturdy scrub brush to clean the perches

- food (a good-quality fresh seed mixture or a formulated diet, such as pellets or crumbles)

- a millet spray (most budgies love this treat!)

- a powdered vitamin and mineral supplement to sprinkle on your pet's fresh foods

- a variety of safe, fun toys

- a cage cover (an old sheet or towel that is free of holes and ravels will serve this purpose nicely)

- a playgym to allow your budgie time out of its cage and a place to exercise

a breeder is willing to show you around his or her facility, consider it a special treat and an honor that few people enjoy.

Bird Shows and Marts

These offer bird breeders and bird buyers an opportunity to get together to share a love for birds. Bird shows can provide prospective bird owners with the chance to see many different types of birds all in one place (usually far more than many pet shops would keep at a time), which can help you narrow your choices if you're undecided about which species to keep. At a bird show, you can watch to see which birds win consistently, then talk to the breeder of these birds after the show to see if he or she expects any chicks. (This is especially important if you decide to get into showing budgies, because you want to start with winning stock.)

A bird mart is a little different than a bird show. At a bird mart, various species of birds and a wide variety of birdkeeping supplies are offered for sale, so you can go and shop to your heart's content.

Pet Stores

Pet stores can be the ideal place to purchase a budgie. You'll have to check with stores in your area to determine if they even sell pets, since many stores chose not to carry livestock beginning in the early 1990s. These will be listed as "pet supply stores" in your phone book and may be the place you'll want to go to get the cage, food, dishes, perches, toys and other accessories you'll need once your budgie comes home.

If a store in your area sells live pets, you'll need to visit the store and make sure it's clean and well kept. Walk around the store a bit. Are the floors clean? Do the cages look and smell like they're cleaned regularly? Do the animals in the cages appear alert, well-fed and healthy? Do the cages appear crowded or do the animals inside have some room to move around?

Did someone greet you when you walked into the store? Is the store staff friendly? Do they seem to care that you came in to shop? Remember that you will be visiting a pet store every week or two to purchase food, toys and other items for your budgie, so you might want to select a store with friendly people behind the counter.

After you've determined that the store is clean and the employees are pleasant, find out if the staff tries to keep their birds healthy. Do they ask you to wash your hands with a mild disinfectant before handling their birds or between birds? If they do, don't balk at the request. This is for the health of the birds, and it indicates that the store is concerned about keeping its livestock healthy. Buying a healthy bird is much easier and more enjoyable than purchasing a pet with health problems, so don't be afraid to follow the rules in a caring store!

When selecting a budgie, choose a healthy, robust bird rather than the shy animal that hides in the corner.

If something about the store, staff or livestock doesn't feel quite right, choose another establishment to do business with. If the store and its livestock meet with your approval (as they often will), then it's time to get down to the all-important task of selecting your budgie.

Choosing the Right Budgie

Look at the budgies that are available for sale. If possible, sit down and watch them for awhile. Don't rush this important step. Do some of them seem bolder than the others? Consider those first, because you want a curious, active, robust pet, rather than a shy animal that hides in a corner. Are other budgies sitting off by themselves, seeming to sleep while their cagemates play? Reject any birds that seem too quiet or too sleepy because these signs can indicate illness.

Remember that healthy birds spend their time doing four main activities—eating, playing, defecating and sleeping—in about equal amounts of time. If you notice that a bird seems to only want to sleep, for instance, reject that bird in favor of another whose routine seems more balanced.

You may think that saving a small, picked-upon budgie from its cage-mates seems like the right thing to do, but please resist this urge. You want a strong, healthy, spirited bird, rather than "the runt of the litter." Although it sounds hard-hearted, automatically reject any birds that are being bullied, are timid or that hide in a corner or shy away from you. It will save you some heartache in the end.

If possible, let your budgie choose you. Many pet stores display their budgies in colony situations on playgyms, or a breeder may bring out a clutch of babies for you to look at. If one bird waddles right up to you and wants to play, or if one comes over to check you out and just seems to want to come home with you, that's the bird you want!

> ## SIGNS OF GOOD HEALTH
>
> Here are some of the indicators of a healthy budgie. Keep them in mind when selecting your pet.
>
> bright eyes
>
> a clean cere (the area above the bird's beak that covers its nares or nostrils)
>
> upright posture
>
> a full-chested appearance
>
> actively moving around the cage
>
> clean legs and vent
>
> smooth feathers
>
> good appetite

MALE OR FEMALE?

As you're selecting your budgie, many questions are probably coming to mind, including the sex of your potential pet and if it needs a companion bird.

You may be asking, "Should I get a male or a female budgerigar?" Although males may make slightly better talkers, I'd encourage you to get a young, healthy bird and enjoy it for its full pet potential. If you have your heart set on an older bird, males generally have blue ceres, while females' ceres are brownish, but don't try this sexing test on a young bird because cere color develops as a bird matures.

ONE OR TWO?

Another question you may have (especially if you have a busy schedule) is "Should I get one bird or two?" Single pet budgies generally make more affectionate pets, because you and your family become the bird's substitute flock. But a pair of budgies can be pretty entertaining as they chase each other around the cage and encourage each other into all sorts of avian mischief.

One small drawback of owning two pet budgies, especially young ones, is that they may have a tendency to chase each other around the cage, playfully tugging on one another's tail feathers. Sometimes these feathers come out, leaving you with two considerably shorter budgies until the next set of tail feathers grows in.

A pair of budgies may be more inclined to bond to each other than to you.

If you have a pair of birds that suddenly become tailless, check the cage bottom for the feathers and watch your birds to see if they do, indeed, chase and pester

each other. If so, you have nothing to worry about. If not, please alert your avian veterinarian to the problem and ask for further guidance. Two birds are also less likely to learn to talk because they can chatter to each other in budgie rather than learning the language of their substitute "flock."

There is also the possibility of territorial behavior on the part of the original bird. This territorial behavior can include bullying the newcomer and keeping him or her away from food and water dishes to the point that the new bird cannot eat or drink.

To avoid this problem, house the birds in separate cages until you can supervise their interactions. Let the birds out together on a neutral playgym and watch how they act with each other. If they seem to get along, you can move their cages closer together so they can become accustomed to being close. Some birds will adjust to having other birds share their cages, while others prefer to remain alone in their cages with other birds close by.

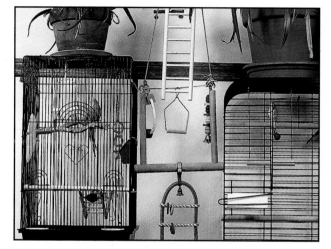

If you are bringing a new budgie into a one-budgie home, keep the birds in separate cages and supervise their interactions until you are sure they have accepted each together.

By the same token, don't try to put a new budgie into the cage of a bird you already own, and don't house budgies with other small birds, such as finches, canaries, cockatiels or lovebirds. Budgies may tend to bully finches and canaries, keeping them away from food and water bowls, while cockatiels and lovebirds may exhibit the same behavior toward budgies.

To keep peace in your avian family, make sure every bird has its own cage, food and water bowls. Some budgies will get along with other birds during supervised playtime on a playgym, while others do not "work and play well with others" and enjoy being the only pets out on the gym.

What Does That Band Mean?

As you select your pet, you may notice leg bands on the budgies you're looking at. Bird bands serve several purposes. First, they help identify a particular breeder's stock. They can also help establish an age for your bird, since many of them have the year of hatch as part of the band's code. Finally, in an effort to reduce the number of smuggled birds that are kept as pets in the United States, some states require that certain pet birds be banded with closed, traceable bands. Although this requirement doesn't apply to budgies, it is an indication of things to come in aviculture.

Bringing Your Budgie Home

QUARANTINE

If you have other birds in your home, you will want to quarantine your budgie for at least thirty days to ensure it doesn't have any diseases that your other birds could catch. To do this, you will need to keep your budgie as far away from your other birds as possible, preferably in a separate room. Feed your newly arrived budgie after you feed your other birds, and be sure to wash your hands thoroughly before and after handling or playing with your new pet. Quarantine is usually just a precautionary measure, but you can't be too safe when your pet's health is involved!

Bands are used to identify a breeder's stock, and are also helpful in preventing the smuggling of birds into the United States.

ADJUSTMENT TIME

Although you will probably want to start playing with your new budgie the minute you bring it home from the breeder, bird mart or store, please resist

this temptation. Your new pet will need some time to

adjust to its new environment, so be patient. Spend the time instead talking quietly to your new pet, and use its name frequently while you're talking. Move slowly around your budgie for the first few days to avoid startling it.

YOUR BUDGIE'S ROUTINE

You will be able to tell when your new pet has settled into its routine. By observation, you will soon recognize your budgie's routine and know what is normal. You may also notice that your bird fluffs or shakes its feathers to greet you, or that it chirps a greeting when you uncover its cage in the morning. If your budgie should learn to talk, it may eventually greet you with a cheery "hello" or "good morning" as you uncover its cage.

Living

with a

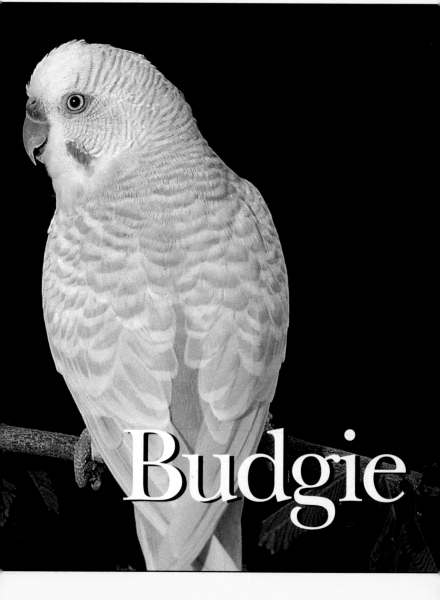

part two

Budgie

chapter 3

Better
Budgie
Care

Ten Steps to Better Bird Care

Bird keeping isn't particularly difficult to do. In fact, if you only do ten things for your budgie for as long as you own it, your bird will have a pretty healthy, well-adjusted life.

Provide an adequate cage in a safe, secure location in your home. The cage should be located in a fairly active part of your home so your bird will feel as if it's part of your family and your daily routine.

Next, clean the cage regularly to protect your pet from illness and to make its surroundings more enjoyable for both of you. Would you want to live in a smelly, dirty house? Your bird doesn't like it either.

Third, clip your bird's wings regularly to ensure its safety. Also bird-proof your home and practice bird safety by closing windows and doors securely before you let your bird out of its cage.

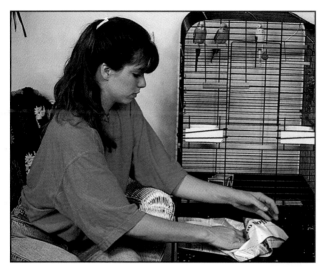

Clean your budgie's cage regularly to protect your pet from illness and to keep its environment pleasant.

Fourth, offer your budgie a varied diet that includes seeds or pellets, fresh vegetables and fruits cut into budgie-sized portions and healthy people food, such as raw or cooked pasta, fresh or toasted whole-wheat bread and unsweetened breakfast cereals.

Your budgie should also have access to clean, fresh drinking water at all times.

Next, establish a good working relationship with a qualified avian veterinarian early on in your bird ownership (preferably on your way home from the pet store or breeder). Don't wait for an emergency to locate a veterinarian.

Sixth, take your budgie to the veterinarian for regular checkups, as well as when you notice a change in its routine. Preventive care helps head off serious problems before they develop.

Seventh, set and maintain a routine for your budgie. Make sure it's fed at about the same time each day, playtime out of its cage occurs regularly and that bedtime is well established.

Eighth, provide an interesting environment for your bird. Entertain and challenge your bird's curiosity with a variety of safe toys. Rotate these toys in and out of your bird's cage regularly, and discard any that become soiled, broken or unsafe.

Ninth, leave a radio or television on for your bird when you are away from home, because a too-quiet environment can be stressful for many birds, and stress can cause illness or other problems for your pet.

Finally, pay attention to your budgie on a consistent basis. Don't lavish abundant attention on the bird when you first bring it home, then gradually lose interest in it. Set

Stimulate your budgie by offering a variety of toys and rotating them in and out of its cage.

aside a portion of each day to spend with your budgie—you'll both enjoy it and your relationship will benefit from it. Besides, wasn't companionship one of the things you were looking for when you picked your budgie as a pet?

Now that doesn't seem too difficult, does it? Just devote a little time each day to your pet bird, and soon the two of you will have formed a lifelong bond of trust and mutual enjoyment.

A Routine for You and Your Budgie

A budgie requires a certain level of care *every day* to ensure its health and well-being. Birds are happiest when they are secure and comfortable in a safe environment. You can help your budgie feel more secure by establishing a daily routine and performing the same rituals at around the same time every day. This way, your budgie knows his needs will be met by the people he considers to be his family. Here are some of the things you'll need to do each day for your pet:

- Observe your pet for any changes in its routine (report any changes to your avian veterinarian immediately).

- Offer fresh food and remove old food. Wash food dish thoroughly with detergent and water. Rinse thoroughly and allow to dry.

- Provide fresh water and remove previous dish. Wash dish as above.

- Change paper in cage tray.

- Let the bird out of its cage for supervised playtime.

Finally, you'll want to cover your bird's cage at about the same time every night to indicate bedtime. When you cover the cage, you'll probably hear your bird rustling around for a bit, perhaps getting a drink of water or a last mouthful of seeds before settling in for the night. Keep in mind that your pet will require eight to ten hours of sleep a day, but you can expect that it will take naps during the day to supplement its nightly snooze.

Let your budgie have quality, out-of-cage time with you daily.

BE ALERT TO HEALTH INDICATORS

Although it may seem a bit unpleasant to discuss, your bird's droppings require daily monitoring because they can tell you a lot about its general health. Budgies will produce small, flat droppings that appear white in the center with a dark green edge. These droppings are usually composed of equal amounts of fecal material (the green edge), urine (the clear liquid portion) and urates (the white or cream-colored center). A healthy budgie generally eliminates between twenty-five and fifty times a day, although your bird may go more or less often.

Texture and consistency, along with frequency or lack of droppings, can let you know how your pet is feeling. For instance, if a bird eats a lot of fruits and vegetables, its droppings are generally looser and more watery than a bird that eats primarily seeds. But watery droppings can also indicate illness, such as diabetes or kidney problems, that causes a bird to drink more water than usual.

> ## WARM WEATHER WARNING
>
> On a warm day, you may notice your bird sitting with its wings held away from its body, rolling its tongue and holding its mouth open. This is how a bird cools itself off. Watch your bird carefully on warm days because it can overheat quickly and may suffer heatstroke, which requires veterinary care. If you live in a warm climate, ask your avian veterinarian how you can protect your bird from this potentially serious problem.

Color can also give an indication of health. Birds that have psittacosis typically have bright, lime-green droppings, while healthy birds have avocado or darker green and white droppings. Birds with liver problems may produce droppings that are yellowish or reddish, while birds that have internal bleeding will produce dark, tarry droppings.

But a color change doesn't necessarily indicate poor health. For instance, birds that eat pelleted diets tend to have darker droppings than their seed-eating companions, while parrots that have splurged on a certain fresh food soon have droppings with that characteristic color. Birds that overindulge on beets, for instance, produce bright red droppings that can look for all the world as though the bird has suffered some serious internal injury. Birds that overdo sweet potatoes, blueberries or raspberries produce orange, blue or red droppings. During pomegranate season, birds that enjoy this fruit develop violet droppings that can look alarming to an unprepared owner.

As part of your daily cage cleaning and observation of your feathered friend, look at its droppings carefully. Learn what is normal for your bird in terms of color, consistency and frequency, and report any changes to your avian veterinarian promptly.

WEEKLY CHORES

Some of a budgie owner's weekly chores will include:

Removing old food from cage bars and from the corners of the cage where it invariably falls.

Removing, scraping and replacing the perches to keep them clean and free of debris (you might also want to sand them lightly with coarse grain sandpaper to clean them further and improve perch traction for your pet).

Rotating toys in your bird's cage to keep them interesting. Remember to discard any toys that show excessive signs of wear (frayed rope, cracked plastic or well-chewed wood).

You can simplify the weekly cage cleaning process by placing the cage in the shower and letting hot water from the shower head do some of the work. Be sure to remove your budgie, its food and water dishes, the cage tray paper and its toys before putting the cage into the shower. You can let the hot water run over the cage for a few minutes, then scrub any stuck-on food with an old toothbrush or some fine-grade steel wool. After you've removed the food and other debris, you can disinfect the cage with a spray-on disinfectant that you can purchase at your pet store. Make sure to choose a bird-safe product, and read the instructions fully before use.

Once a week, thoroughly clean your budgie's cage.

Rinse the cage thoroughly and dry it completely before returning your bird and its accessories to the cage. (If you have wooden perches in the cage, you can dry them more quickly by placing the wet dowels in a 400-degree oven for 10 minutes. Let the perches cool before you put them back in the cage.)

Let your budgie cool down in hot weather with a spray of clean water.

SEASONAL NEEDS

Warm weather requires a little extra vigilance on your part to ensure that your pet remains comfortable. To help keep your pet cool, keep it out of direct sun, offer it lots of fresh, juicy vegetables and fruits (be sure to remove these fresh foods from the cage promptly to prevent your bird from eating spoiled food) and mist it lightly with a clean spray bottle (filled with water only) that is used solely for showers.

By the same token, pay attention to your budgie's needs when the weather turns cooler. You may want to use a heavier cage cover, especially if you lower the heat in your home at bedtime, or you may want to move the bird's cage to another location in your home that is warmer or less drafty.

TRAVELING WITH YOUR BIRD

As your budgie becomes part of your family, you will need to know how to deal with it in every aspect of family life. When I worked for *Bird Talk,* we often heard from owners who wanted to take their pets on vacation and people relocating to another state or country who had to take their bird with the rest of the family. The advice we gave depended on the owner and his or her pet. These were some of the questions we asked:

Does the bird like new adventures?

Is there a trusted relative or friend that you can leave the bird with while you are away?

Does your avian veterinarian's office offer boarding?

How long will you be gone?

Will you be visiting a foreign country?

If the owners were going on a family vacation, we usually recommended leaving the bird at home in familiar surroundings with its own food, water and cage or in the care of a trusted friend, relative, pet-sitter or avian veterinarian.

We did this because birds are creatures of habit that like their routines, and because taking birds across state lines or international boundaries is not without risk. Some species are illegal in certain states (Quaker, or monk, parakeets, for example, which are believed to pose an agricultural threat to some states because of their hearty appetites) and some foreign countries have lengthy quarantine stays for pet birds. It was our professional opinion that, although it would be difficult to leave your bird behind, it was better for the bird.

Should you choose to leave your pet at home while you're away, you have several care options available to you. First, you can recruit the services of a trusted friend or relative, which is an inexpensive and convenient solution for many pet owners. You can return the pet-sitting favor for your friend or relative when he or she goes out of town.

If your trusted friends and relatives live far away, you can hire a professional pet-sitter (many advertise in the yellow pages, and some offer additional services, such as picking up mail, watering your plants and leaving lights and/or radios on to make your home look occupied while you're gone). If you're unsure about what to look for in a pet-sitter, the National Association of Pet-Sitters offers the following tips:

Look for a bonded pet-sitter who carries commercial liability insurance. Ask for references and for a written description of services and fees.

Arrange to have the pet-sitter come to your home before you leave on your trip to meet the pets and discuss what services you would like him or her to perform while you're away. During the initial interview, evaluate the sitter. Does he or she seem comfortable with your bird? Does the sitter have experience caring for birds? Does he or she own birds?

Ask for a written contract and discuss the availability of vet care (does he or she have an existing arrangement with your veterinarian, for example) and what arrangements the sitter makes in the event of inclement weather or personal illness.

HOLIDAY PRECAUTIONS

The holidays bring their own special set of stresses, and they can also be hazardous to your budgie's health. Drafts from frequently opening and closing doors can have an impact on your bird's health, and the bustle of a steady stream of visitors can add to your pet's stress level (as well as your own).

Chewing on holiday plants, such as poinsettia, holly and mistletoe, can make your bird sick, as can chewing on tinsel or ornaments. Round jingle-type bells can sometimes trap a curious bird's toe, beak or tongue, so keep these holiday decorations out of your bird's reach. Watch your pet around strings of lights, too, as both the bulbs and the cords can prove to be great temptations to curious beaks.

Discuss what the sitter's policy is for determining when a pet owner has returned home. Does he or she visit the home until the owners return? Will he or she call to ensure you've arrived home safely and your pets are cared for, or will you have to call and notify the sitter?

If the prospect of leaving your bird with a pet-sitter doesn't appeal to you, you may be able to board your bird at your avian vet's office. Of course, you'll need to determine if your vet's office offers boarding services and if you want to risk your bird's health by exposing it to other birds during boarding.

I have used the services of trusted friends and my avian veterinarians' offices, and have been equally pleased on both counts. In some cases, my friends were experienced bird owners, while others were simply animal lovers who enjoyed the company of my pet as much as I did. When leaving my bird with my avian vet, I felt that he was in good hands. If something happened to him or if he fell ill, he was in the right place to be taken care of, and if he had an uneventful few days, he still had six or seven people catering to his every whim instead of only me.

chapter 4

Bringing Your
Budgie
Home

Before you bring your feathered friend home, determine where it will live in your house or apartment. Selecting your budgie's cage will be one of the most important decisions you will make for your pet, and where that cage will be located in 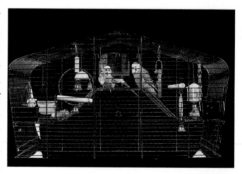 your home is equally important. Don't wait until you bring your bird home to think this through. You'll want your new pet to settle in to its surroundings right away, rather than adding to its stress by relocating it several times before selecting the right spot for the cage.

Choosing a Cage

Although we didn't do too many things right for my childhood budgie, Charlie, we did select a good home for him. Charlie's cage was large, it had both horizontal and vertical bars for his climbing enjoyment, its food and water dishes slid in and out through holes in the side of the cage (which meant they were easy to get to and made his cage simple to service), it had three or four perches placed at different heights in the cage and it had a bedsheet for a cover at night.

Some of the cages you'll look at while making your selection are designed to sit on tabletops, while others have built-in or attached stands. Consider which will work best in your home. If yours is an active house with other pets and children in it, a tabletop cage may be better than a cage with a stand that could be knocked over. If you live alone in a small apartment, a cage and stand might be in order. If you do choose a cage with a stand, be sure the stand is steady and fits well with the cage.

Make sure the bars of your bird's cage are close enough together that your budgie will not get his head stuck between them.

SIZE IS IMPORTANT

When choosing your budgie's cage, remember that it must be large enough to house your bird, its food and water bowls, perches and toys. *Bird Talk* columnist Susan Chamberlain recommends that budgie owners "test cages for 60," which means that the measurements of the cage's length, width and height should total at least 60 when added together. A common size for budgie cages is 18 inches wide, 18 inches high and 24 inches long, which adds up to 60. This would be about the smallest cage to consider if you own a single pet bird. If you have more than one bird or if your bird is an upwardly mobile creature with lots of belongings (toys, food dishes, a bathtub perhaps), a larger cage is in order.

Simply put, buy the largest cage you can afford, because you don't want your pet to feel cramped. Remember, too, that budgies are like little airplanes, flying horizontally, rather than little helicopters that hover up and down. For this reason, long rectangular cages that offer horizontal space for short flights are preferred to high, narrow cages that don't provide much flying room.

ACRYLIC OR WIRE?

Birdcages are traditionally made of wire, but you may see acrylic cages in magazine advertisements or at your local pet store. These cages are better at containing seed hulls, loose feathers and other debris your bird creates, which may make bird-keeping easier and more enjoyable for you. This is a plus if you want to keep your home clean of birdie debris while still enjoying your pet birds.

Before they moved to Texas with their owners, I regularly bird-sat a pair of Pacific parrotlets that had a tendency to fling food around with the greatest of ease. When they were kept in a traditional wire cage, my dining room table and walls bore lasting reminders of each visit no matter how diligently I scrubbed them. When the birds returned later in an acrylic cage, nothing remained to mark their passing after their owners took them home. I also bird-sit a canary that lives in an acrylic cage. It is the easiest bird I have ever cleaned up after, because the feathers, seed hulls and treat scraps remain contained within the cage. All I have to do for this bird is change the cage paper daily and service its food and water bowls twice a day. My own bird's wire cage, on

CAGE CONSIDERATIONS
Your budgie will spend much of its time in its cage, so make this environment as stimulating, safe and comfortable as possible. Keep the following things in mind when choosing a good cage for your budgie.
• Make sure the cage is big enough. The dimensions of the cage (height, length and depth) should add up to 60 for a single bird.
• An acrylic cage may mean easier clean-up for the bird owner. Wood or bamboo cages will be quickly destroyed by an eager budgie's beak.
• Make sure the cage door opens easily and stays securely open and closed. Avoid "guillotine-style" doors.
• The cage tray should be regularly shaped and easy to slide in and out. There should be a grille covering the cage floor so you can change the substrate without worrying about the bird's escape.

the other hand, requires frequent vacuumings and diligent care.

Although it sounds like a sales pitch, I can attest that acrylic cages clean up easily with a damp towel and regular changing of the tray that slides under the cage itself. If you choose an acrylic cage for your pet, make sure it has numerous ventilation holes drilled in its walls to allow for adequate air circulation. Be particularly careful about not leaving your budgie in direct sunlight if you choose to house it in an acrylic cage, since these cages can get warm rather quickly and your bird could become overheated. (Budgies in wire cages shouldn't be left in direct sunlight either, as they can overheat, too.)

If you find wooden or bamboo cages during your shopping excursions, reject them immediately unless the wood is lined with wire or wire mesh. A busy budgie beak will make short work of a wooden or bamboo cage, and you'll be left with the problem of finding a new home for your pet! These cages are designed for finches and other songbirds that are less likely to chew on their homes than a budgie.

If you choose a wire cage, examine it carefully before making your final selection. Make sure that the finish is not chipped, bubbled or peeling, because a curious budgie may find the spot and continue removing the finish. This can cause a cage to look old and worn before its time, and some cages may start to rust without their protective finishes. Finally, if your budgie ingests any of the finish, it could become ill.

Reject any cages that have sharp interior wires or wide bar spacing. (Recommended bar spacing for budgies is between 3/8 and 7/16 inch.) It could become caught between bars that are slightly wider than recommended, or it could escape through widely spaced bars. Also be aware that some birds may injure themselves on ornate scrollwork that decorates some cages. Finally, make sure the cage you choose has some horizontal bars in it so your budgie will be able to climb the cage walls easier if it wants to exercise.

Cage Door Options

Once you've checked the bar spacing and the overall cage quality, your next concern should be the cage door. Does it open easily for you, yet remain secure enough to keep your bird in its cage when you close the door? Is it wide enough for you to get your hand in and out of the cage comfortably? Will your bird's food bowl or a bowl of bath water fit through it easily? Does the door open up, down or to the side? Some bird owners prefer that their pets have a play porch on a door that opens drawbridge style, while others are happy with doors that open to the side. Watch out for guillotine-style doors that slide up and over the cage entrance, because some budgies have suffered broken legs when the door dropped on them unexpectedly.

Cage Tray Considerations

Next, look at the cage tray. Does it slide in and out of the cage easily? Remember that you will be changing the paper in this tray at least once a day for the rest of your bird's life (about 15 years with good care). Is the tray an odd shape or size? Will paper need to be cut into unusual shapes to fit in it, or will paper towels, newspapers or clean sheets of used computer paper fit easily into it? The easier the tray is to remove and reline, the more likely you will be to change the lining of the tray daily. Can the cage tray be replaced if it becomes damaged and unusable? Ask your pet store staff or the cage manufacturer's customer service department before making your purchase.

Let me briefly address cage substrate or what to put in the cage tray. I recommend clean black-and-white newsprint, paper towels or clean sheets of used computer printer paper. Sand, ground corncobs or walnut shells may be sold by your pet supply store, but I don't recommend these as cage flooring materials because they tend to make owners lazy in their cage cleaning habits. These materials tend to hide feces and discarded food quite well. This can cause a bird owner to forget to change the cage tray on the principle that if it doesn't look dirty, it must not be dirty. This line of thinking can set up a thriving, robust colony of bacteria in the bottom of your bird's cage, which can lead to a sick bird. Newsprint and other paper products don't hide the dirt; in fact, they seem to draw attention to it, which leads conscientious bird owners to keep their pets' homes scrupulously clean.

A cage that has an easily removable, regularly shaped tray will be easier to clean and reline daily.

On a related note, you may see sandpaper or "gravel paper" sold in some pet stores as a cage tray liner. This product is supposed to provide a budgie with an opportunity to ingest grit, which is purported to help aid digestion by providing coarse grinding material that will help break up food in the bird's gizzard. The problem is that experts are unable to agree on just how much grit a pet bird needs. Many British avicultural books advocate offering a budgie regular supplements of grit, while American budgie fanciers are less generous with their offerings because some budgies have overeaten grit that is offered to them. This causes impacted crops, a serious condition that requires immediate veterinary attention. Additionally, if a bird stands on rough sandpaper when it's on the cage floor, it could become prone to infections and other foot problems from the rough surface of the paper. For your budgie's health, please don't use these gravel-coated papers.

Cage Floor

Finally, check the floor of the cage you've chosen. Does it have a grille that will keep your bird out of the debris that falls to the bottom of the cage, such as feces, seed hulls, molted feathers and discarded food? To ensure your pet's long-term good health, it's best to have a grille between your curious pet and the remains of its day in the cage tray. Also, it's easier to keep your budgie in its cage while you're cleaning the cage tray if there's a grille between the cage and the tray.

SPECIAL HOUSING NEEDS

Some budgies have special caging requirements. A budgie I know named Calvin was handicapped as a chick. (I think his mother sat on him too tightly in the nest and squashed his developing skeleton a bit.) As a result of injuries he suffered early in life, Calvin didn't perch too well and had trouble getting around in and living in a conventional wire bird cage.

His owner searched through pet stores to find the best cage for her physically challenged pet, and her solution was a wire hamster cage with climbing ramps and resting platforms, rather than traditional perches. Because the platforms and ramps were wide and had both horizontal and vertical bars on them, Calvin could maneuver around his cage pretty well.

THE CAGE COVER

One important, but sometimes overlooked, accessory is the cage cover. Be sure that you have something to cover your budgie's cage with when it's time to put your pet to sleep each night. The act of covering the cage seems to calm many pet birds and convince them that it's really time to go to bed although they may hear the sounds of an active family evening in the background.

A sheet, towel or blanket makes an effective cage cover.

You can purchase a cage cover, or your can use an old sheet, blanket or towel that is clean and free of holes. Be aware that some birds like to chew on their cage covers through the cage bars. If your bird does this, replace the cover when it becomes too holey to do its job effectively. Replacing a well-chewed cover will also help keep your bird from becoming entangled in the cover or caught in a ragged clump of threads.

WHERE TO PUT THE CAGE

Now that you've picked the perfect cage for your pet, where will you put it in your home? Your budgie will be happiest when it can feel like it's part of the family, so the living room, family room or dining room may be among the best places for your bird. If your budgie is a child's pet, it may do well living in its young owner's room. (Parents should still check on the budgie,

This is an example of a very stressful cage situation. Keep your budgie's cage away from windows and out of reach of curious cats.

though, to ensure that it's being fed and watered regularly and that its cage is clean.) Whatever room you choose, keep the cage out of direct sunlight and make sure that the cage is placed up against a solid wall so that your budgie doesn't become stressed by feeling that its home is exposed on all sides.

Avoid keeping your budgie in the bathroom or kitchen, though, because sudden temperature fluctuations or fumes from cleaning products used in those rooms could harm your pet. Another spot to avoid is a busy hall or entryway, because the activity level in these spots may be too much for your pet.

Additional Supplies

Along with the perfect-sized cage in the ideal location in your home, your pet will need a few cage accessories. These include food and water dishes, perches and toys.

FOOD AND WATER DISHES

When selecting dishes for your budgie, be sure to pick up several sets so that mealtime cleanups are quick and easy. Choose only uncovered dishes for your pet's food and water because budgies are often reluctant to stick their heads into hooded feeders to eat. Some have even starved to death rather than eat from a covered dish. Be sure to check your bird's seed dish daily to make sure that it has seeds, rather than just empty seed hulls in the dish, and refill when necessary.

PERCHES

When choosing perches for your pet's cage, try to buy two different diameters or materials so your bird's feet won't get tired of standing on the same-sized perch of the same material day after day. Think of how tired your feet would feel if you stood on a piece of wood in your bare feet all day, then imagine how it would feel to stand on that piece of wood barefoot everyday for 10 or 15 years. Sounds pretty uncomfortable, doesn't it? That's basically what your bird has to look forward to if you don't vary its perching choices.

The recommended diameter for budgie perches is 1/2 inch, so try to buy one perch that's this size and one that is slightly larger (5/8 inch, for example) to give your pet a chance to stretch its foot muscles. Birds spend almost all of their lives standing, so keeping their feet healthy is important. Also, avian foot problems, such as bumblefoot or pressure sores on the soles of the feet, are much easier to prevent than they are to treat after they've become a problem.

A perch placed toward the top of the cage will serve as a sleeping roost for your budgie.

When you walk down the bird-care aisle at your local pet store, you'll probably notice that a variety of perch materials are available to bird owners. Along with the traditional wooden dowels are manzanita branches, PVC tubes, rope perches, and terra-cotta or concrete grooming perches. Each has its advantages.

Manzanita offers birds varied diameters on the same perch, along with chewing possibilities, while PVC is pretty indestructible. (Make sure any PVC perches you offer your bird have been scuffed slightly with sandpaper to improve traction.) Rope perches also offer varied diameters and a softer perching surface than wood or plastic, and terra-cotta and concrete provide slightly abrasive surfaces that birds can use to groom their beaks without severely damaging the skin on their feet in the process. Some bird owners have reported that their pets have suffered foot abrasions with these perches, however; watch your budgie carefully for signs of sore feet (signs may include an inability to perch or climb, favoring a foot or raw, sore skin on the feet) if you choose to use these perches in your pet's cage. If your bird shows signs of lameness, remove the abrasive perches immediately and arrange for your avian veterinarian to examine your bird.

To further help your bird avoid foot problems, do not use sandpaper covers on its perches. These sleeves, touted as nail trimming devices, really do little to trim a parrot's nails because birds don't usually drag their nails along their perches. What the sandpaper perch covers are good at doing, though, is abrading the surface of your budgie's feet, which can leave them vulnerable to infections and can make movement painful.

When placing perches in your budgie's cage, try to vary the heights slightly so your bird has different "levels" in its cage. Don't place any perches over food or water dishes, because birds will contaminate food or water by defecating in it. Finally, place one perch higher than the rest for a nighttime sleeping roost. Budgies and other parrots like to sleep on the highest point they can find to perch, so please provide this security to your pet.

Because perches can sometimes double as chew toys, don't be alarmed if your budgie suddenly seems to become a feathered termite. It may need more chew toys in its cage, or it may just like destroying perches. In either case, be prepared to make many trips to your pet store for replacement toys and perches, and be glad that you have a healthy, well-adjusted pet that likes to play.

Choosing the Right Toys

When selecting toys for your pet, keep a few safety tips in mind.

Size

First, is the toy the right size for your bird? Large toys can be intimidating to small birds, which makes the birds less likely to play with them. On the other end of the spectrum, larger parrots can easily destroy toys designed for smaller birds, and they can sometimes injure themselves severely in the process.

Safety

Next, is the toy safe? Good choices include sturdy wooden toys (either undyed or painted with bird-safe vegetable dye or food coloring) strung on closed-link chains or vegetable-tanned leather thongs, and rope toys. If you purchase rope toys for your budgie, make sure its nails are trimmed regularly to prevent them from snagging in the rope, and discard the toy when it becomes frayed to prevent accidents.

Unsafe items to watch out for are brittle plastic toys that can be shattered into fragments easily by a budgie's busy beak, lead-weighted toys that can be cracked open to expose the dangerous lead to curious birds, loose link chains that can catch toenails or beaks, ring toys that are too small to climb through safely, or jingle-type bells that can trap toes, tongues or beaks.

A homemade toy of toilet paper tubes will delight your budgie.

SOCIAL CONCERNS

Mirrors are found on many budgie toys, and most birds are fascinated with and enamored of that handsome pet in the reflection. Some birds become so infatuated with "the other bird" that they seem to lose interest in their owners, so you might want to wait until your budgie is settled in its surroundings and comfortable with you before adding a mirrored toy to its cage.

HOMEMADE TOYS

Some entertaining toys can be made at home. Give your budgie an empty paper towel roll or toilet paper tube (from unscented paper only, please), string some Cheerios on a piece of vegetable-tanned leather or offer your bird a dish of uncooked pasta pieces to destroy.

In the wild, silence indicates the presence of a predator. Keep your budgie relaxed by playing music or leaving the TV on while you are away from the house.

When you're putting toys in your budgie's cage for the first time, you might want to leave the toy next to the cage for a few days before actually putting it in the cage. Some birds accept new items in their cages almost immediately, but others need a few days to size up a new toy, dish or perch before sharing cage space with it.

NOISE COMPANY

Earlier, I mentioned the importance of having a radio or television on for your budgie if you leave it home alone for long periods of time. Although budgies have been kept as pets for about 150 years, they may still instinctively harken back to their wild roots at times. In the grasslands of Australia as in the jungles of Latin America and Africa, silence usually indicates a predator in the area, which can raise a bird's stress level. Because you don't want a stressed-out pet, please leave a radio or television on for your budgie if you will be away so that it will have some background noise and some variety in its daily routine. Some budgies may even learn the words to commercial jingles they hear on the radio or TV!

The Playgym

Although your budgie will spend quite a bit of time in its cage, it will also need time out of its cage to exercise and enjoy a change of scenery. A playgym can be just what your budgie needs to keep it physically and mentally active.

If you visit a large pet store or bird specialty store, or look through the pages of any pet bird hobbyist magazine, you will see a variety of playgyms on display. You can choose a complicated gym with a series of ladders, swings, perches and toys, or you can purchase a simple T-stand that has a place for food and water bowls and an eyescrew or two from which you can hang toys. If you're really handy with tools, you can even construct a gym to your budgie's size and playing specifications.

A playgym will help to keep your budgies physically and mentally stimulated.

As with the cage, the location of your budgie's playgym will be a consideration. You will want the gym placed in a secure location in your home that is safe from other curious pets, ceiling fans, open windows and other household hazards. You will also want the gym to be in a spot frequented by your family, so your bird will have company and supervision while it plays.

chapter 5

Feeding
Your
Budgie

People do not live by bread alone, and birds can't prosper on a diet of seeds and water. Think how dull and unhealthy a one-item diet would be for you—it isn't any more interesting for your budgie.

Poor diet also causes a number of health problems (respiratory infections, poor feather condition, flaky skin, reproductive problems, to name a few) and is one of the main reasons some budgies live fairly short lives. Let's look again at my childhood pet, who ate basically a seed-and-water diet and lived about five years. If we had offered him a more varied diet, Charlie could have lived three times that long.

A Healthy Diet

Here's what the Association of Avian Veterinarians recommends as a healthy budgie diet: 50 percent seed, grain and legumes; 45 percent dark green or dark orange vegetables and fruits; and 5 percent meat (well cooked, please), eggs (also well cooked) or dairy products. We'll look at each part of this diet in a little more detail in just a moment.

Whatever healthy fresh foods you offer your budgie, be sure to remove any leftover food from the cage promptly to prevent spoilage and to help keep your bird healthy. Ideally, you should change the food in your bird's cage every two to four hours (about every thirty minutes in warm weather), so a budgie should be all right with a tray of food to pick through in the morning, another to select from during the afternoon and a fresh salad to nibble on for dinner.

SEEDS AND GRAINS

The seeds, grain and legumes portion of your budgie's diet can include clean, fresh seed from your local pet supply store. Give your pet its seeds in a clean, dry dish, and check the dish daily to ensure your budgie has enough food. Don't just look in the dish, but actually remove it from the cage and blow lightly into the dish (you might want to do this over the kitchen sink or the trash can) to remove seed hulls. Budgies are notorious for giving the impression that they have enough food. Because they are such neat eaters and drop the used hulls right back in their dishes, they can often fool you.

Seeds along with fruits and vegetables are the major components of a nutritious budgie diet.

One foodstuff that is very popular with budgies is millet, especially millet sprays. These golden sprays are part treat and part toy. Offer your budgie this treat sparingly, however, because it is high in fat and can make your budgie pudgy! Other items in the bread group that you can offer your pet include unsweetened breakfast cereals, whole-wheat bread, cooked beans, cooked rice and pasta.

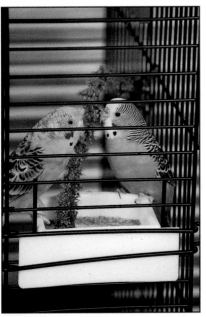

Millet sprays are a budgie favorite, but offer them sparingly because they are high in fat.

FRUITS AND VEGETABLES

Dark green or dark orange vegetables and fruits contain vitamin A, which is an important part of a bird's diet and is missing from the seeds, grains and legumes group. This vitamin helps fight off infection and keeps a bird's eyes, mouth and respiratory system healthy. Some vitamin-A-rich foods are carrots, yams, sweet potatoes, broccoli, dried red peppers, dandelion greens and spinach.

You may be wondering whether or not to offer frozen or canned vegetables and fruits to your bird. Some birds will eat frozen vegetables and fruits, while others turn their beaks up at the somewhat mushy texture of these foodstuffs. The high sodium content in some canned foods may make them unhealthy for your budgie. Frozen and canned foods will serve your bird's needs in an emergency, but I would offer only fresh foods on a regular basis.

PROTEIN

Along with small portions of the well-cooked meat I mentioned earlier, you can also offer your budgie bits of tofu, water-packed tuna, fully scrambled eggs, cottage cheese, unsweetened yogurt or low-fat cheese. Don't overdo the dairy products, though, because a bird's digestive system lacks the enzyme lactase, which means it is unable to fully process dairy foods.

Taboos

Now that we've looked at foods that are good for your bird, let's look briefly at those that aren't healthy for your budgie. **_Do not feed_** alcohol, rhubarb or avocado (the skin and the area around the pit can be toxic) to your pet. Don't give your budgie any foods that are highly salted, sweetened or fatty (such as pretzels, candy or potato chips). Especially do not give your bird chocolate because it contains a chemical, theobromine, that birds cannot digest as completely as people can. Chocolate can kill your budgie, so resist the temptation to share this snack with your pet. You will also want to avoid giving your bird seeds or pits from apples, apricots, cherries, peaches, pears and plums, because they contain toxins that can be harmful to your pet's health.

Vegetables provide necessary amounts of vitamin A, a required nutrient missing from a seed diet.

Sharing People Food

Let common sense be your guide in choosing which foods can be offered to your bird: If it's healthy for you, it's probably okay to share. However, remember to reduce the size of the portion you offer to your bird—a few shreds of grated carrot or squash, a single Cheerio or a few cooked beans will be more appealing to your budgie than a larger, human-sized portion.

Sharing healthy people food with your budgie is completely acceptable, but sharing something that you've already taken a bite of is not. Human saliva has bacteria in it that are perfectly normal for people but that are potentially toxic to birds, so please don't share partially eaten food with your pet. For your bird's health and your peace of mind, get it a separate portion or plate.

By the same token, please don't kiss your budgie on the beak (kiss it on top of its little head instead) or allow your budgie to put its head into your mouth, nibble on your lips or preen your teeth. Although you may see birds doing this on television or in pictures in a magazine and think that it's a cute trick, it's really unsafe for your bird's health and well-being.

Try offering budgie-sized portions of nutritious people food to your pet.

Enticing the Older Budgie

If you've adopted an older budgie that eats primarily seeds, try offering your bird some of the fruits and vegetables that are popular with many parrots, such as apple slices, grapes or corn. You can offer a small slice of apple that you've dipped in seeds, a halved grape or some fresh corn kernels (offering a slice of corn on the cob is also an option). Although these fruits and vegetables are not as rich in important vitamins as their dark green or dark orange counterparts, they can help bridge the gap between seeds and a more varied diet for fussy eaters. To ease the stress of relocating to your home, try to feed your budgie a diet as close to the one it ate in its previous home. To help your bird adjust even faster, you may want to sprinkle some food on the cage floor, because budgies sometimes revert to their natural ground-feeding habits in times of stress.

The Pelleted Diet Option

Just what is a pellet anyway, you're probably thinking. Don't birds just eat seeds? While seeds are an important part of many birds' diets, some budgie owners prefer to feed their pets a pelleted diet rather than a mixture of seeds, vegetables, fruits and healthful table food.

Pelleted diets are created by mixing a variety of healthful ingredients into a mash and then forcing (or extruding) the hot mixture through a machine to form various shapes. Some pelleted diets have colors and flavors added, while others are fairly plain. These formulated diets provide more balanced nutrition for your pet bird in an easy-to-serve form that reduces the amount of wasted food and eliminates the chance for a bird to pick through a smorgasbord of healthful foods to find its favorites and reject the foods it isn't particularly fond of. Some budgies accept pelleted diets quickly, while others require some persuading.

If you want to convert your pet to a pelleted diet, you will want to offer it pellets alongside or mixed with its current diet. (Make sure the budgie recognizes that pellets are food before proceeding.) Once you see that your bird is eating the pellets, begin to gradually increase the amount of pellets you offer at mealtime while decreasing the amount of other food you serve. Within a couple of weeks, your bird should be eating its pellets with gusto!

If your budgie seems a bit finicky about trying pellets, you may have to make it believe that you enjoy pellets as a snack. Really play up your apparent enjoyment of this new food because it will pique your budgie's curiosity and make the pellets exceedingly interesting to your pet.

SPROUTING

You can test the seed for freshness by sprouting some of them in some water on your windowsill. Soak the seeds thoroughly with water and drain the excess. In two or three days, fresh seeds will sprout; stale seeds won't. After the fresh seeds sprout, you can rinse them well and feed them to your budgies, too. Immediately discard any sprouts that smell funny or grow mold; these are unhealthy to feed to your budgie.

If you have another bird in the house that already eats a pelleted diet, place your budgie's cage where it can watch the other bird enjoy its pellets. Before long, your budgie will be playing "follow the leader" right to the food bowl. Finally, you may want to roll a favorite treat, such as a damp broccoli floret or an apple slice, in pellets and offer this decorated piece of produce to your pet.

Whatever you do, don't starve your bird into trying a new food. Offer a variety of new foods consistently, along with familiar favorites. This will ensure that your bird is eating and will also encourage it to try new foods. Don't be discouraged if your budgie doesn't dive right in to a new food. Be patient, keep offering new foods to your bird and praise it enthusiastically when it is brave enough to sample something new!

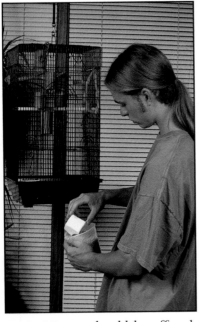

A pelleted diet offers a full complement of vitamins and minerals. You may have to be patient and ingenious to get your budgie to accept it.

Grit

As a new bird owner, you may hear a lot of talk about the importance of grit in your bird's diet. Birds use grit in their gizzards to grind their food, much as we use our teeth. How much grit birds need and how often it should be offered to them is a source of contention among avian veterinarians and bird breeders. Some will tell you birds need grit regularly, while others will advise against it. If your budgie's breeder and your avian veterinarian think your bird requires grit, offer it sparingly (only about a pinch every few weeks). Do not offer it daily, and do not provide your budgie with a separate dish of grit because some birds will overeat the grit and suffer dangerous crop impactions as a result.

Supplements

You may also be concerned if your bird is receiving adequate amounts of vitamins and minerals in its diet. This is of particular concern if your budgie is eating a seed-based diet. Budgies on pelleted or formulated diets should have all their vitamin and mineral needs met with these special diets, so additional supplements are unnecessary. If your budgie's diet is mainly seeds, however, you may want to sprinkle a good-quality vitamin-and-mineral powder onto your pet's fresh foods, where it has the best chance of sticking to the food and being eaten. Vitamin-enriched seed diets may provide some supplementation, but some of them add the vitamins and minerals to the seed hull, which your pet will remove and discard while it's eating. Avoid adding vitamin and mineral supplements to your budgie's water dish, because they can act as a growth medium for bacteria. They may also cause the water to taste different to your bird, which could discourage it from drinking.

YOUR BUDGIE'S BEAK

Because budgies eat primarily seeds and other plant materials (in the wild (some budgies have been seen eating the seeds of 21 different species of grasses), their beaks have developed into efficient little seed crackers. Look at the underside of your bird's upper beak. It has tiny ridges in it that help your budgie hold and crack seeds more easily.

chapter 6

Grooming
Your
Budgie

Your budgie has several grooming needs. It must be able to bathe regularly, and it will need to have its nails and flight feathers trimmed periodically to ensure its safety.

Although some people would say that a budgie's beak also needs trimming, I would argue that a healthy bird that has enough chew toys seems to do a remarkable job of keeping its beak trimmed. If your budgie's beak becomes overgrown, though, please consult your avian veterinarian. A parrot's beak contains a surprising number of blood vessels, so beak trimming is best left to the experts. Also, a suddenly overgrown beak may indicate that your bird is suffering from liver damage, a virus or scaly mites, all of which require veterinary care.

A healthy bird with plenty of chew toys is unlikely to need a beak trim. If you think your budgie does, consult your veterinarian.

Preening

This is one of your budgie's ways of keeping itself well-groomed. You will notice it ruffling and straightening its feathers each day. It will also take oil from the gland at the base of its tail and spread it on the rest of its feathers, so don't be concerned if you see your budgie apparently pecking or biting at its tail. Preening, combined with your assistance in bathing, nail clipping and wing clipping will keep your budgie in top shape.

Bathing Your Budgie

You can bathe your budgie in a variety of ways. You can mist it lightly with a clean spray bottle filled with warm water only, or you can allow it to bathe in the kitchen or bathroom sink under a slow stream of water. Many budgies prefer to bathe in their cages, either in a small flat saucer of warm water, a plastic budgie bathtub or an

Preening is the way your bird naturally grooms itself.

*Budgies like to
bathe in any
number of ways.
This one is
enjoying its bath
in a special
budgie bathtub.*

enclosed bird bath that you can purchase in your local pet store. Bathing is important to birds to help them keep their feathers clean and healthy, so don't deny your pet the chance to bathe!

Unless your budgie has gotten itself into oil, paint, wax or some other substance that elbow grease alone won't remove and that could harm its feathers, it will not require soap as part of its bath. Under routine conditions, soaps and detergents can damage a bird's feathers by removing beneficial oils, so hold the shampoo during your budgie's normal clean-up routine!

Let your bird bathe early in the day so it has an opportunity to let its feathers dry completely during the day. In cooler weather, you may want to help the process along by drying your budgie off with a blow dryer to prevent it from becoming chilled after its bath. To do this, set the blow dryer on low and keep it moving so that your bird doesn't become overheated. Your budgie may soon learn that drying off is the most enjoyable part of its bath!

Nail Trimming

Trimming your budgie's nails is a fairly simple procedure. Budgies and other parrots need their nails clipped occasionally to prevent the nails from catching on toys or perches and injuring themselves. Unlike some of the larger parrots, budgie nails are light in color, which makes it easier for owners to see where the nail stops and the blood and blood supply (or quick) begins. In budgies, the quick is generally seen as a pink color inside the nail.

You will need to remove only tiny portions of the nail to keep your budgie's claws trimmed. Generally, a good guideline to follow is to only remove the hook on each nail, and to do this in the smallest increments possible. Stop well before you reach the quick. If you do happen to cut the nail short enough to make it bleed, apply cornstarch or flour, followed by direct pressure, to stop the bleeding.

Wing Trimming

The goal of a properly done wing trim is to prevent your pet from flying away or flying into a window, mirror or wall while it's out of its cage. An added benefit of trimming your pet's wings is that its inability to fly well will make it more dependent on you for transportation, which should make it easier to handle. However, the bird still needs enough wing feathers so that it can glide safely to the ground if it is startled and takes flight from its cagetop or playgym.

Because this is a delicate procedure, you may want to enlist the help of your avian veterinarian, at least the first time. Wing trimming is a task that must be performed carefully to avoid injuring your pet, so take your time if you're doing it yourself. Please *do not* just take up the largest pair of kitchen shears you own and start snipping away, because I have had avian veterinarians tell me about budgies whose owners cut off their birds' wing tips (down to the bone) in this manner.

To trim the right length off your budgie's nails, cut only the hook at the end of each nail.

The first step in wing feather trimming is to assemble all the things you will need and find a quiet, well-lit place to groom your pet before you catch and trim it. Your grooming tools will include

- a washcloth or small towel to wrap your budgie in

- small, sharp scissors to do the actual trimming

61

- needle-nosed pliers (to pull any blood feathers you may cut accidentally)

- flour or cornstarch to act as styptic powder in case a blood feather is cut

- nail trimmers (while you have your bird in the towel, you might as well do its nails, too)

Larger parrots require an assistant trimmer to hold the bird while the trimmer clips the wing feathers, but budgies are small enough for one person to handle.

I encourage you to groom your pet in a quiet, well-lit place because grooming excites some birds and causes them to become wiggly. Having good light to work under will make your job easier, and having a quiet work area may just calm down your pet and make it a bit easier to handle.

Once you've assembled your supplies, drape the towel over your hand and catch your budgie with your toweled hand. Grab your bird by the back of its head and neck, and wrap it in the towel. Hold your bird's head securely with your thumb and index finger. (Having the bird's head covered by the towel will calm it and will give it something to chew on while you clip its wings.)

Lay the bird on its back, being careful not to constrict or compress its chest (remember, birds have no diaphragms to help them breathe) and spread its wing out carefully to look for new feathers that are still growing in, also called blood feathers. These can be identified by their waxy, tight look (new feathers in their feather sheaths resemble the end of a shoelace) and their dark centers or quills, which are caused by the blood supply to the new feather.

If your bird has a number of blood feathers, you may want to put off trimming its wings for a few days,

---

GROOMING TIPS

Groom your pet in a quiet, well-lit place.

Have all the necessary grooming supplies close by before you begin.

Make sure you have styptic powder on hand.

Check wings and toenails regularly to see if they need retrimming.

---

because older, fully grown feathers act as a cushion to protect those just coming in from life's hard knocks. If your bird has only one or two blood feathers, you can trim the full-grown feathers accordingly. *Never trim a blood feather.*

To trim your bird's feathers, separate each one away from the other flight feathers and cut it individually (remember, the goal is to have a well-trimmed bird that's still able to glide a bit if it needs to). Use the primary coverts (the set of feathers above the primary flight feathers on your bird's wing) as a guideline as to how short you should trim.

Trim the first five to eight primary flight feathers on each wing.

Cut the first five to eight flight feathers starting from the tip of the wing, and be sure to trim an equal number of feathers from each wing. Although some people think that a bird needs only one trimmed wing, this is incorrect and could actually cause harm to a bird that tries to fly with one trimmed and one untrimmed wing. Think of how off balance that would make you feel; your budgie is no different.

If you do happen to cut a blood feather, remain calm. You must remove it and stop the bleeding to ensure that your bird doesn't bleed to death, and panicking will do neither of you much good.

To remove a blood feather, take a pair of needle-nosed pliers and grasp the broken feather's shaft as close to

63

the skin of your bird's wing as you can. With one steady motion, pull the feather out completely. After you've removed the feather, put a pinch of flour or cornstarch on the feather follicle (the spot you pulled the feather out of) and apply direct pressure for a few minutes until the bleeding stops. If the bleeding doesn't stop after a few minutes of direct pressure, or if you can't remove the feather shaft, contact your avian veterinarian for further instructions.

Although it may seem like you're hurting your budgie by removing the broken blood feather, consider this: A broken blood feather is like an open faucet. If left in, the faucet stays open and lets the blood out. Once removed, the bird's skin generally closes up behind the feather shaft and shuts off the faucet.

Now that you've successfully trimmed your bird's wing feathers, congratulate yourself. You've just taken a great step toward keeping your bird safe. But don't rest on your laurels just yet; you must remember to check your budgie's wing feathers and retrim them periodically (about four times a year as a minimum).

Molting

At least once a year, your budgie will lose its feathers. Don't be alarmed, because this is a normal process called molting. I say at least once because many pet birds seem to be in a perpetual molt, with feathers falling out and coming in throughout the summer.

You can consider your bird in molting season when you see a lot of whole feathers in the bottom of the cage and you notice that your bird seems to have broken out in a rash of stubbly little aglets (those plastic tips on the ends of your shoelaces). These are the feather sheaths that help new pinfeathers break through the skin, and they are made of keratin (the same material that makes up our fingernails). The sheaths helps protect growing feathers from damage until the feather completes its growth cycle.

You may notice that your budgie is a little more irritable during the molt; this is to be expected. Think about how you would feel if you had all these itchy new feathers coming in all of a sudden. However, your bird may actively seek out more time with you during the molt because owners are handy to have around when a budgie has an itch on the top of its head that it can't quite scratch! (Scratch these new feathers gently because some of them may still be growing in and may be sensitive to the touch.) Some birds may benefit from special conditioning foods during the molt; check with your avian veterinarian to see if your bird is a candidate for these foods.

Be particularly alert after a molt, because your bird will have a whole new crop of flight feathers that need attention. You'll be able to tell when your budgie is due for a trim when it starts becoming bolder in its flying attempts. Right after a wing trim, a budgie generally tries to fly and finds it's unsuccessful at the attempt. It will keep trying, though, and may surprise you one day with a fairly good glide across its cage or from its play-gym. If this happens, get the scissors and trim those wings immediately. If you don't, the section that follows on finding lost birds may have more meaning than you can imagine.

If Your Bird Escapes

As we discuss wing trimming, it is as good a time as any to discuss the possibility of your bird escaping. One of the most common accidents that befalls bird owners is that a fully flighted bird escapes through an open door or window. Just because your bird has never flown before or shown any interest in leaving its cage doesn't mean that it can't fly or that it won't become disoriented once it's outside. If you don't believe it can happen, just check the lost and found advertisements in your local newspaper for a week. Chances are many birds will turn up in the lost column, but few are ever found.

Why do lost birds never come home? Some birds fall victim to predatory animals in the wild, while others join flocks of feral, or wild, parrots (Florida and California are particularly noted for these). Still other

65

lost birds end up miles away from home because they fly wildly and frantically in any direction. And the people who find them don't advertise in the same area that the birds were lost in. Finally, some people who find lost birds don't advertise that they've been found because the finders think that whoever was unlucky or uncaring enough to lose the bird in the first place doesn't deserve to have it back.

How can you prevent your bird from becoming lost? First, make sure its wings are safely trimmed at regular intervals. Be sure to trim both wings evenly and remember to trim wings after your bird has molted.

Next, be sure your bird's cage door locks securely and that its cage tray cannot come lose if the cage is knocked over or dropped accidentally. Also be sure that all your window screens fit securely and are free from tears and large holes. Keep all window screens and patio doors closed when your bird is at liberty. Finally, don't ever go outside with your bird on your shoulder.

If your bird does fly away, use an open, inviting cage, and a tape of the bird's voice played outside to lure it home.

If, despite your best efforts, your bird should escape, you must act quickly for the best chance of recovering your pet. Here are some things to keep in mind:

> If possible, keep the bird in sight. This will make chasing it easier.

> Have an audiotape of your bird's voice and a portable tape recorder available to lure your bird back home.

> Place your bird's cage in an area where your bird is likely to see it, such as on a deck or patio. Put lots of treats and food on the floor of the cage to tempt your pet back into its home.

Use another caged bird to attract your budgie's attention.

Alert your avian veterinarian's office that your bird has escaped. Also let the local humane society and other veterinary offices in your area know.

Post fliers in your neighborhood describing your bird. Offer a reward and include your phone number.

Don't give up hope.

Are Mite Protectors Necessary?

While we're discussing grooming and feather care, I'd like to suggest that you not purchase mite protectors that hang on a bird's cage or conditioning products that are applied directly to a bird's feathers. Well-cared-for budgies don't have mites and shouldn't be in danger of contracting them. (If your pet does have mites, veterinary care is the most effective treatment method.) Also, the fumes from some of these products are quite strong and can be harmful to your pet's health. Conditioners, anti-picking products and other substances that are applied to your bird's feathers will serve one purpose: to get your bird to preen itself so thoroughly in an effort to remove the offending liquid from its feathers that it could remove all its feathers in a particular area. If you want to encourage your bird to preen regularly and help condition its feathers, simply mist the bird regularly with clean, warm water or hold it under a gentle stream from a kitchen or bathroom faucet. Your bird will take care of the rest.

chapter 7

Your Budgie's Physical Health

Avian Anatomy

If you think your body doesn't have much in common with your pet budgie's, you'd be wrong. You both have skin; skeletons; respiratory, cardiovascular, digestive, excretory and nervous systems; and sensory organs, although the various systems function in slightly different ways.

SKIN

Your budgie's skin is probably pretty difficult to see since your pet has so many feathers. If you part the feathers carefully, though, you can see your pet's thin, transparent skin and the muscles beneath it. Modified skin cells help make up your bird's beak, cere, claws and the scales on its feet and legs.

Skeletal System

Next, let's look at your bird's skeleton. Did you know that some bird bones are hollow? This makes them lighter and flying easier, but it also means that these bones can be more susceptible to breakage. For this reason, you must always handle your bird carefully! Another adaptation for flight is that the bones of a bird's wing (which correspond to our arm and hand bones) are fused for greater strength.

Birds have air sacs in some of their bones (these are called pneumatic bones) that help lighten their bodies for flight. They also have air sacs throughout their bodies to cool them more efficiently. Birds cannot perspire as mammals do because birds have no sweat glands, so they must have a way to cool off.

Parrots have ten neck vertebrae to human's seven. This makes a parrot's neck more free moving than a person's (a parrot can turn its head almost 180 degrees), which can be advantageous to spotting food or predators in the wild.

During breeding season, a female bird's bones become denser as they store calcium needed to create eggshells. A female's skeleton can weigh up to 20 percent more during breeding season than it does the rest of the year because of this calcium storage.

Respiratory System

Your bird's respiratory system is a highly efficient system that works in a markedly different way from yours. Here's how your budgie breathes: Air enters the system through your bird's nares, passes through its sinuses and into its throat. As it does, the air is filtered through the **choana,** which is a slit that can be easily seen in the roof of many birds' mouths. The choana also helps to clean and warm the air before it goes further into the respiratory system.

After the air passes the choana, it flows through the larynx and trachea, past the **syrinx** or "voice box." Your bird doesn't have vocal cords like you do; rather, vibration of the syrinx membrane is what allows our birds to make sounds.

So far it sounds similar to the way we breathe, doesn't it? Well, here's where the differences begin. As the air continues its journey past the syrinx and into the bronchi, your bird's **lungs** don't expand and contract to bring the air in. This is partly due to the fact that birds don't have diaphragms like people do. Instead, the bird's body wall expands and contracts, much like a fireplace bellows. This action brings air into the air sacs I mentioned earlier. This bellows action also moves air in and out of the lungs.

Although a bird's respiratory system is extremely efficient at exchanging gases in the system, two complete breaths are required to do the same work that a single breath does in people and other mammals. This is why you may notice that your bird seems to be breathing quite quickly. The average respiratory rate for a budgerigar is between sixty-five and eighty-five breaths per minute (compare this to the average twelve to sixteen breaths per minute a person takes).

CARDIOVASCULAR SYSTEM

Along with the respiratory system, your bird's cardiovascular system keeps oxygen and other nutrients moving throughout your pet's body, although the circulatory path in your budgie differs from yours. In your budgie, blood flowing from the legs, reproductive system and lower intestines passes through the kidneys on its way back to the general circulatory system.

Like you, though, your budgie has a four-chambered heart, with two atria and two ventricles. Unlike your average heart rate of seventy-two beats per minute, your budgie's average heart rate is 350 to 550 beats per minute. According to Dr. Gary Gallerstein, cardiac output (the amount of blood pumped through the heart in a minute) in a flying budgerigar is seven times greater than in a human exercising at maximum capability! Having such efficient respiratory and circulatory systems allows budgerigars and other parrots to use incredible amounts of energy very efficiently.

Digestive System

To keep this energy-efficient machine (your bird's body) running requires fuel (or food). This is where your bird's digestive system comes in. One of the main functions of the digestive system is to provide the fuel that maintains your bird's body temperature.

Your budgie's digestive system begins with its **beak.** The size and shape of a bird's beak depend on its food-gathering needs. Compare and contrast the sharp, pointed beak of an eagle or the elongated bill of a hummingbird with the small, hooked beak of your budgie.

A parrot's mouth works a little differently than a mammal's. Parrots don't have saliva to help break down and move their food around like we do. Also, their taste buds are contained in the roofs of their mouths. Because they have few taste buds, experts think that a parrot's sense of taste is poorly developed.

After the food leaves your bird's mouth, it travels down the **esophagus,** where it is moistened. The food then travels to the **crop,** where it is moistened further and is supplied in small increments to the bird's stomach.

After the food leaves the crop, it travels through the **proventriculus,** where digestive juices are added, to the **gizzard,** where the food is broken down into even smaller pieces. The food then travels to the **small intestine,** where nutrients are absorbed into the bloodstream. Anything that's leftover then travels through the large intestine to the **cloaca,** which is the common chamber that collects wastes before they leave the bird's body through the vent. The whole process from mouth to vent usually takes only a few hours, which is why you may notice that your bird leaves frequent, small droppings in its cage.

Along with the solid waste created by the digestive system, your budgie's kidneys create urine, which is then transported through ureters to the cloaca for excretion. Unlike a mammal, a bird does not have a bladder or a urethra.

Nervous System

Your budgie's nervous system is very similar to your own. Both are made up of the brain, the spinal cord and countless nerves throughout the body that transmit messages to and from the brain.

Now that we've examined some of the similarities between avian and human anatomy, let's stop and look at some of the unusual anatomical features birds have. The first feature I'd like to discuss is probably one of the reasons you're attracted to birds: feathers. Birds are the only animals that have feathers, which serve several purposes. Feathers help birds fly, they keep birds warm, they attract the attention of potential mates, and they help scare away predators.

Feathers

Did you know that your budgie has between 2,000 and 3,000 feathers on its body? These feathers grow from follicles that are arranged in rows known as pterylae. The unfeathered patches of bare skin on your budgie's body are called apteria.

A feather is a remarkably designed creation. The base of the feather shaft, which fits into the bird's skin, is called the quill. It is light and hollow, but remarkably tough. The upper part of the feather shaft is called the rachis. From it branch the barbs and barbules (smaller barbs) that make up most of the feather. The barbs and barbules have small hooks on them that enable the different parts of the feather to interlock like Velcro and form the feather's vane or web.

Birds have several different types of feathers on their bodies. **Contour feathers** are the colorful outer feathers on a bird's body and wings. Many birds have an undercoating of down feathers that helps keep them warm. **Semiplume feathers** are found on a bird's beak, nares (nostrils) and eyelids.

A bird's flight feathers can be classified into one of two types. **Primary flight feathers** are the large wing feathers that push a bird forward during flight. They are also the ones that need clipping (see Chapter 6, "Grooming Your Budgie," for more information on clipping wings). **Secondary flight feathers** are found on the inner wing, and they help support the bird in flight. Primary and secondary wing feathers can operate independently of each other. The bird's tail feathers also assist in flight by acting as a brake and a rudder to make steering easier.

Feather colors are determined by combinations of pigment in the outer keratin layer and in the interior structure of the feather.

To keep their feathers in good condition, healthy birds will spend a great deal of time fluffing their feathers and preening them. You may see your budgie seeming to pick at the base of its tail on the topside. This is a normal behavior in which the bird removes oil from the preen gland and spreads it on its feathers. The oil also helps prevent skin infections and waterproofs the feathers.

Sometimes pet birds will develop white lines or small holes on the large feathers of their wings and tails. These lines or holes are referred to as "stress bars" or "stress lines" and result from the bird experiencing stress as the feathers were developing. If you notice stress bars on your budgie's feathers, discuss them with your avian veterinarian.

Your budgie has between 2,000 and 3,000 feathers on its body.

BUDGIE SENSES

Sight

Although I mentioned earlier that a bird has a poor sense of taste, it has a well-developed sense of sight. Birds can see detail and they can discern colors. Be aware of this when selecting cage accessories for your pet, because some budgies react to a change in the color of their food dishes. Some seem excited by a different color bowl, while others act fearful of the new item.

Because their eyes are located on the sides of their heads, most pet birds rely on monocular vision, which means that they use each eye independently of the other. If a bird really wants to study an object, you will often see it tilt its head to one side and examine the object with just one eye. Birds aren't really able to move their eyes around very much, but they compensate for this by having highly mobile necks that allow them to turn their heads about 180 degrees.

Like cats and dogs, birds have third eyelids called nictitating membranes that you will sometimes see flick briefly across your budgie's eye. The purpose of this membrane is to keep the eyeball moist and clean. If you see your budgie's nictitating membrane for more than a brief second, please contact your avian veterinarian for an evaluation.

You have probably noticed that your bird lacks eyelashes. In their place are small feathers called semiplumes that help keep dirt and dust out of the bird's eyeballs.

Hearing

You may be wondering where your budgie's ears are. Look carefully under the feathers behind and below each eye to find them. The ears are the somewhat large holes in the sides of your budgie's head. Budgies have about the same ability to distinguish sound waves and determine the location of the sound as people do, but birds seem to be less sensitive to higher and lower pitches than their owners.

Taste and Smell

You may be wondering how your budgie's senses of smell and taste compare to your own. Birds seem to have poorly developed senses of smell and taste because smells often dissipate quickly in the air (where flying birds spend their time) and because birds have fewer taste buds in their mouths than people do.

(Parrot taste buds are located in the roof of the birds' mouths, not in the tongue like ours are.)

Touch

The final sense we relate to, touch, is well-developed in parrots. Parrots use their feet and their mouths to touch their surroundings (young birds particularly seem to "mouth" everything they can get their beaks on), to play and to determine what is safe to perch on or chew on and what's good to eat.

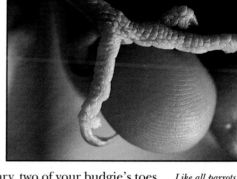

Along with their tactile uses, a parrot's feet also have an unusual design compared to other caged birds. Look at your budgie's feet, and compare them to a finch, softbill or canary. Do you notice that, unlike a finch or canary, two of your budgie's toes point forward and two point backward? This two toes forward and two toes back arrangement is called zygodactyl, and it allows a parrot to climb up and down, and around in trees easily. Some larger parrots also use their feet to hold food or to play with toys.

Like all parrots, budgies have four toes—two pointing forward and two pointing backward.

Visiting the Veterinarian

With good care, a budgerigar can live up to eighteen years, although the average life span of these small parrots is about one-third of that, or six years. One of the reasons budgies don't live longer is that their owners may be reluctant to take their pets to the veterinarian. Some people don't want to pay veterinary bills on such "inexpensive" birds.

Choosing a Veterinarian

As a caring owner, you want your bird to have good care and the best chance at living a long, healthy life.

To that end, you will need to locate a veterinarian who understands the special medical needs of birds and one with whom you can establish a good working relationship. The best time to do this is when you first bring your budgie home from the breeder or pet store. If possible, arrange to visit your veterinarian's office on your way home from the breeder or store. This is particularly important if you have other birds at home, because you don't want to endanger the health of your existing flock or your new pet.

If you don't know an avian veterinarian in your area, ask the person from whom you bought your budgie where he or she takes his or her birds. (Breeders and bird stores usually have avian veterinarians on whom they depend.) Talk to other bird owners you know and find out who they take their pets to, or call bird clubs in your area for referrals.

If you have no bird-owning friends or can't locate a bird club, your next best bet is the yellow pages. Read the advertisements for veterinarians carefully, and try to find one who specializes in birds. Many veterinarians who have an interest in treating birds will join the Association of Avian Veterinarians and advertise themselves as members of this organization. Some veterinarians have taken and passed a special examination that entitles them to call themselves avian specialists.

Once you've received your recommendations or found likely candidates in the telephone book, start calling

SIGNS OF ILLNESS

To help your veterinarian and to keep your pet from suffering long-term health risks, keep a close eye on its daily activities and appearance. If something suddenly changes in the way your bird looks or acts, contact your veterinarian immediately. Birds naturally hide signs of illness to protect them from predators, so by the time a bird looks or acts sick, it may already be dangerously ill.

Some signs of illness include

- a fluffed-up appearance
- a loss of appetite
- sleeping all the time
- a change in the appearance or number of droppings
- weight loss
- listlessness
- drooping wings
- lameness
- the bird has partially eaten food stuck to its face or food has been regurgitated onto the cage floor
- labored breathing, with or without tail bobbing
- runny eyes or nose
- the bird stops talking or singing

If your bird shows any of these signs, please contact your veterinarian's office immediately.

the veterinary offices. Ask the receptionist how many birds the doctor sees in a week or month, how much an office visit costs, and what payment options are available (cash, credit card, check or time payments). You can also inquire if the doctor keeps birds as his or her personal pets.

If you like the answers you receive from the receptionist, make an appointment for your budgie to be evaluated. (If you don't, of course, move on to the next name on your list.) Make a list of any questions you want to ask the doctor regarding diet, how often your bird's wings and nails should be clipped or how often you should bring the bird in for an examination.

Plan to arrive a little early for your first appointment because you will be asked to fill out a patient information form. This form will ask you for your bird's name, its age and sex, the length of time you have owned it, your name, address and telephone number, your preferred method of paying for veterinary services, how you heard about the veterinary office and the name and address of a friend the veterinary office can contact in case of emergency. The form may also ask you to express your opinion on the amount of money you would spend on your pet in an emergency, because this can help the doctor know what kind of treatment to recommend in such instances.

WHAT THE VETERINARIAN MAY ASK YOU

Bird owners should not be afraid to ask their avian veterinarians questions. Avian vets have devoted a lot of time, energy and effort to studying birds, so put this resource to use whenever you can.

What bird owners may not know is that they may be asked a number of questions by the veterinarian. When you take your bird in for an exam, be aware that the doctor may ask you for answers to these questions:

- Why is the bird here today?

- What's the bird's normal activity level like?

- How is the bird's appetite?

- What does the bird's normal diet consist of?

- Have you noticed a change in the bird's appearance lately?

Be sure to explain any changes in as much detail as you can, because changes in your bird's normal behavior can indicate illness.

During the initial examination, the veterinarian will probably take his or her first look at your budgie while it is still in its cage or carrier. The doctor may talk to you and your bird for a few minutes to give the bird an opportunity to become accustomed to him or her, rather than simply reaching right in and grabbing your pet. While the veterinarian is talking to you, he or she will check the bird's posture and its ability to perch.

Next, the doctor should remove the bird from its carrier or cage and look it over carefully. He or she will particularly note the condition of your pet's eyes, its beak and its nares (nostrils). The bird should be weighed, and the veterinarian will probably palpate (feel) your budgie's body and wings for any lumps, bumps or deformities that require further investigation. Feather condition will also be assessed, as will the condition of the bird's vent, legs and feet.

COMMON AVIAN VETERINARY TESTS

After your veterinarian has completed your budgie's physical examination, he or she may recommend further tests. These can include:

- Blood workups help a doctor determine if your bird has a specific disease. Blood tests can be further broken down into a complete blood count, which determines how many platelets, red and white blood cells your bird has (this information can help diagnose infections or anemia), and a blood chemistry profile, which helps a veterinarian analyze how your bird's body processes enzymes, electrolytes and other chemicals.

- Radiographs or x-rays allow a veterinarian to study the size and shape of a bird's internal organs, along with the formation of its bones. X-rays also help doctors find foreign bodies in a bird's system.

- Microbiological exams help a veterinarian determine if any unusual organisms (bacteria, fungi or yeast) are growing inside your bird's body.

- Fecal analysis studies a small sample of your bird's droppings to determine if it has internal parasites, or a bacterial or yeast infection.

Once the examination is concluded and you've had a chance to discuss any questions you have with your veterinarian, the doctor will probably recommend a follow-up examination schedule for your pet. Most healthy birds visit the veterinarian annually, but some have to go more frequently.

Medicating Your Budgie

Most bird owners are faced with the prospect of medicating their pets at some point in the birds' lives, and many are unsure if they can complete the task without hurting their pets. If you have to medicate your pet, your avian veterinarian or veterinary technician should explain the process to you. In the course of the explanation, you should find out how you will be administering the medication, how much of a given drug you will be giving your bird, how often the bird needs the medication and how long the entire course of treatment will last.

If you find (as I often have) that you've forgotten one or more of these steps after you arrive home, call your vet's office for clarification to ensure that your bird receives the follow-up care from you that it needs.

ORAL MEDICATION

This is a good route to take with birds that are small, easy to handle or underweight. The medication is usually given with a needleless plastic syringe placed in the left side of the bird's mouth and pointed toward the right side of its throat. This route is recommended to ensure that the medication gets into the bird's digestive system and not into its lungs, where aspiration pneumonia can result.

Medicating a bird's food or offering medicated feed (such as tetracycline-laced pellets that were fed to imported birds during quarantine to prevent psittacosis) is another effective possibility, but medications added to a bird's water supply are often less effective because sick birds are less likely to drink water, and the medicated water may have an unusual taste that makes a bird less likely to drink it.

If you need to administer oral medication to your budgie, use an oral syringe to make sure the medication gets into the digestive system.

INJECTED MEDICATION

Avian veterinarians consider this the most effective method of medicating birds. Some injection sites—into a vein, beneath the skin or into a bone—are used by avian veterinarians in the clinic setting. Bird owners are usually asked to medicate their birds intramuscularly, or by injecting medication into the bird's chest muscle. This is the area of the bird's body that has the greatest muscle mass, so it is a good injection site.

It's perfectly understandable if you're hesitant about giving your bird shots. I was the first time I had to medicate my bird this way, but we both survived the procedure. Wrap your bird securely, but comfortably, in a washcloth or small towel, and lay it on your lap with its chest up. Hold its head securely with your thumb and index finger of one hand, and use the other to insert the syringe at about a 45 degree angle under the bird's chest feathers and into the muscle beneath.

You should remember to alternate the side you inject your bird on (say, left in the morning and right in the evening) to ensure that one side doesn't get overinjected and sore, and you should remain calm and talk to your bird in a soothing tone while you're administering the drugs. Before you both know it, the shot is over and your bird is one step closer to a complete recovery!

TOPICAL MEDICATION

This method, which is far less stressful than the one we just discussed, provides medication directly to part of a bird's body. Uses can include medications for eye infections, dry skin on the feet or legs or sinus problems.

My bird and I are living proof that all the methods described above work and are survivable by both bird and owner. He has received oral and injectable antibiotics for recurring infections, and he has had topical ointments applied to his feet to clear up a dry skin problem. Although I would have doubted that I would be able to give him injections when I first adopted him seven years ago, I now know that I can do it with a minimal amount of stress for both of us.

Budgie Health Concerns

Although budgies are generally hardy birds, they are prone to a few health problems, including scaly face, goiter, gout, obesity and lipomas. They, like all birds, can also suffer from respiratory problems and other conditions that result from a vitamin-A deficiency, especially if they consume diets that are high in seeds and low in vitamin-A-rich foods. Vitamin-A deficiency can be prevented by feeding a varied, healthy diet.

SCALY FACE

Scaly face is a condition caused by the *Knemidokoptes* mite, a tiny relative of the spider that likes to burrow into the top layers of a budgie's skin around its cere, eyelids, vent or legs. This burrowing leaves white crusts on the bird's cere or the corners of the mouth. If allowed to progress, scaly face can cause lesions on a bird's beak, eyelids, throat, vent, legs and feet.

81

Advanced cases can also cause beak deformation and horny appendages on a bird's face and legs. The leg appendages can interfere with a bird's ability to move its legs and toes.

If your avian veterinarian suspects your budgie has scaly face, he or she will diagnose the condition by examining skin scrapings under a microscope. Although scaly face has the potential to be a serious condition, the good news is that it can be easily treated by a veterinarian using Ivermectin, which will remove the mites and restore the skin to its normal appearance.

Although some over-the-counter remedies are sold to treat scaly face, a veterinarian-supervised course of treatment using Ivermectin will clear up the problem more quickly and easily than using a nonprescription product.

GOITER

Goiter is an enlargement of the thyroid gland in a bird's throat. It is caused by an iodine deficiency and is most often seen in budgies that eat seed-only diets. Symptoms include difficulty in breathing and swallowing, and regurgitation. Your veterinarian can determine if your budgie has a goiter through x-rays and blood tests. Iodine supplements are used to treat the condition.

GOUT

Gout is associated with kidney problems. Specifically, gouty birds have kidneys that are unable to remove excess nitrogen from the bird's bloodstream. This causes uric acid and urates to build up in the bird's body or in its joints. The exact cause of gout is unclear at this time, but high levels of dietary sodium or calcium and inadequate fluid intake may contribute to gout.

Two forms of gout occur: articular gout, which affects a bird's lower leg joints as shiny, cream-colored swellings, and visceral gout, which affects a bird's internal organs and is difficult to diagnose. Articular gout, the type most often seen in budgies, is a painful condition that causes an affected bird to go lame.

Presently, no cure exists for gout. Treatment includes lowering protein levels and increasing the amount of fruits and vegetables in the bird's diet, along with treating any underlying infections that may have an impact on kidney function. Veterinarians may be able to lower a bird's uric acid levels with medication, and they can also prescribe drugs to ease the bird's pain. Padded perches also seem to offer comfort to afflicted birds.

OBESITY

Obesity can sometimes be caused by a malfunctioning thyroid gland, but it is most often caused by a bird eating far more calories than it burns in a day. (English budgies seem to be more prone to obesity than their American cousins.) To prevent this from happening to your pet budgie, make sure that it eats a well-balanced diet that is low in oil seeds and nuts (sunflower seeds, millet, peanuts, walnuts) and that it receives ample opportunity to exercise both inside its cage and outside of it during supervised "out times" on a playgym.

If your budgie is overweight, you may notice that it has developed a fatty growth, or lipoma, that may impair its ability to fly. Some experts think that these lipomas are linked to a lack of exercise in pet budgies. The good news is that most lipomas can be removed safely by your veterinarian.

BUMBLEFOOT

This is an infection of the sole of the bird's foot. It can cause redness and inflammation, swelling and lameness. Antibiotics, bandages and surgery may be needed to treat the condition, which can be prevented by keeping a bird's cage clean and feeding it a well-balanced diet.

GIARDIA

This illness is caused by a protozoan called *Giardia psittaci*. This organism may cause a bird to have loose droppings, lose weight, pick its feathers, lose its appetite and become depressed. Diagnosing this disease can be tricky, because the *Giardia* organism is difficult to detect in a bird's feces. The disease can be spread through contaminated food or water, and birds are not immune to it once they've had it. Your veterinarian can recommend an appropriate medication to treat *Giardia*.

FRENCH MOULT

This condition causes flight and tail feathers to develop improperly or not develop at all. Researchers believe the disease is caused by polyomavirus, which can be spread through contact with new birds, as well as from feather and fecal dust.

Adult birds can carry polyomavirus but not show any signs of the disease. These seemingly healthy birds can pass the virus to young birds that have never been exposed, and these young birds can die from polyomavirus rather quickly. Sick birds can become weak, lose their appetites, bleed beneath the skin, have enlarged abdomens, become paralyzed, regurgitate and have diarrhea. Some birds with polyomavirus suddenly die.

At present, there is no cure, although a vaccine is under development. Protecting your pets against polyomavirus and other diseases is why it's important to quarantine new stock and to take precautions, including showering and changing clothes, before handling your pet when you've gone to other bird owners' homes, to bird marts that have large numbers of birds from different vendors on display or to bird specialty stores with unhealthy stock.

PAPILLOMA

Papillomas are benign tumors that can appear almost anywhere on a bird's skin, including its foot, leg, eyelid or preen gland. If a bird has a papilloma on its cloaca, the bird may appear to have a "wet raspberry" coming out of its vent. These tumors, which are caused by a virus, can appear as small, crusty lesions, or they may be raised growths that have a bumpy texture or small projections.

Many papillomas can be left untreated without harm to the bird, but some must be removed by an avian veterinarian because a bird may pick at the growth and cause it to bleed.

PSITTACINE BEAK AND FEATHER DISEASE SYNDROME (PBFDS)

This virus has been a hot topic among birdkeepers for the last decade. It was first detected in cockatoos and was originally thought to be a cockatoo-specific problem. It has since been determined that more than forty species of parrots, including budgerigars, can contract this disease, which causes a bird's feathers to become pinched or clubbed in appearance. Other symptoms include beak fractures and mouth ulcers. This highly contagious, fatal disease is most common in birds less than three years of age, and there is no cure at present. A vaccine is under development at the University of Georgia.

Household Hazards

One of the reasons you chose a budgie as a pet is because it's such a curious, active little bird. This curiosity and activity can lead your pet into all sorts of mischief around your home, some of which can be harmful to your bird.

This doesn't mean you shouldn't let your pet out of its cage. On the contrary, all parrots need time out of their cages to maintain physical and mental health. The key to keeping your pet safe and healthy is to watch over it and play with it when it's out of its cage. Both of you will come to enjoy these playtimes greatly.

Some household hazards to be aware of (dangers to budgies are included in parenthesis) include:

- unscreened windows and doors (escape potential)

- mirrors (collision and injury potential)

- exposed electrical cords (possible electrocution if chewed on)

- toxic houseplants (poisoning)

- unattended ashtrays (burns from lit cigarettes or poisoning from ingesting cigarette butts)

- venetian blind cords (hanging)

- sliding glass doors (open: escape potential/closed: collision and injury potential)

- ceiling fans (injury potential)

- open washing machines, dryers, refrigerators, freezers, ovens or dishwashers (bird flies into, is trapped and forgotten, and dies when appliance is activated)

- open toilet bowls (drowning)

- uncovered fish tanks (drowning)

- leaded stained glass items or inlaid jewelry (poisoning)

- uncovered cooking pots on the stove (drowning/scalding/poisoning/burns potential)

- crayons and permanent markers (poisoning)

- pesticides, rodent killers and snail bait (poisoning)

- untended stove burners (burns)

- candles (burns)

- open trash cans (injury by flying into and possibly being tossed out with the trash)

Parrot-proofing your home is akin to baby-proofing it. If you consider that the average macaw or cockatoo is intellectually and emotionally a perpetual two year old, you'll have some idea of the responsibility parrot owners take on when they adopt their pets. Although your budgie is smaller than a cockatoo or a macaw, it is no less curious than its larger cousins and no less precious to you than those larger birds are to their owners, so be aware of the potential dangers found in your home.

The dangers don't stop with the furniture and accessories. A plethora of fumes can overpower your pet, too, such as those from cigarettes, air fresheners, insecticides, bleach, shoe polish, oven cleaners, kerosene, lighter fluid, model and instant glues, active self-cleaning ovens, hairspray, overheated nonstick cookware, paint thinner, bathroom cleaners or nail polish remover. Try to keep your pet away from anything that has a strong chemical odor, and be sure to apply makeup and hair care products far away from your budgie.

To help protect your pet from harmful chemical fumes from cleaning products, consider using "green" alternatives, such as baking soda and vinegar to clear clogged drains, baking soda instead of scouring powder, lemon juice and mineral oil to polish furniture, and white vinegar and water as a window cleaner. Not only will you help your budgie stay healthy, you'll make the environment healthier, too!

Aloe vera is a safe plant for budgies.

Home remodeling and improvement projects can also cause harm to your pet budgie. Fumes from paint or formaldehyde, which can be found in carpet backing, paneling and particle board, can cause pets and people to become ill. If you are having work done on your home, consider boarding your budgie at your avian veterinarian's office or at the home of a bird-loving friend or relative until the project is complete and the house is aired out fully. You can consider the house safe for your pet when you cannot smell any trace of any of the products used in the remodeling.

Another potentially hazardous situation arises when you have your home chemically treated for insects. Ask your exterminator for information about the types of chemicals that will be used in your home, and inquire if pet-safe formulas are available.

If you need to have your home fumigated for termites, for example, ask about treatments, such as electrical currents or liquid nitrogen, which harm the pests without harming your bird. If your house must be treated chemically, arrange to board your bird at your avian veterinarian's office or with a friend before, during and after the fumigation to ensure that no harm comes to your budgie. Make sure your house is aired out completely before bringing your bird home, too.

If you have other pets in the home that require flea treatments, consider pyrethrin-based products. These natural flea killers are derived from chrysanthemums and, although they aren't as long-lasting as synthetic substitutes, they do knock down fleas quickly and are safer in the long run for your pets and you. Or you can treat your dog or cat's sleeping area with diatomaceous earth, which is the crushed shells of primitive one-celled algae. This dust kills fleas by mechanical means, which means that fleas will never develop a resistance to it as they could with chemical products.

Other pets can be harmful to your budgie's health, too. A curious cat could claw or bite your pet, a dog could step on it accidentally or bite it or another, larger bird could break its leg or rip off its upper mandible with its beak. If your budgie tangles with another pet in your home, contact your avian veterinarian immediately because emergency treatment (for bacterial infection from a puncture wound or shock from being stepped on or suffering a broken bone) may be required to save your budgie's life.

Owners and other people can unintentionally be a budgie's worst enemy. At *Bird Talk*, we frequently heard from distraught owners who accidentally rolled over on their pets while bird and owner took a nap together because the owner thought it would be cute to have the bird sleep with him or her. Another common problem grief-stricken owners alerted us to countless times was the danger of leaving nonstick cookware on the stove and having it boil dry because the person forgot about the pot. In the process, toxic fumes were released that killed a beloved pet bird.

Other owners would call, wanting someone to listen to their confession of accidentally stepping on a treasured pet or closing it in the refrigerator, freezer, washer or dryer. Fortunately, in the case of the appliance stories, the bird's disappearance was usually noted before any damage was done.

Marathon cooking sessions may result in overheated cookware or stovetop drip pans, which could kill your bird if the cookware or drip pans are coated with a nonstick finish. (You may want to consider replacing your nonstick cookware with stainless steel pots and pans or glass cookware, which you can treat with a nonstick cooking spray to make cleanups safe and easy.) By the same token, the self-cleaning cycle on some ovens can create harmful fumes for pet birds. Use this cycle only if you've opened the windows around your bird's cage to let in fresh air. (Make sure your budgie's cage is closed securely before opening a window.)

Budgie First Aid

Sometimes your pet will get itself into a situation that will require quick thinking and even quicker

---

PLANTS TO LOOK OUT FOR

Even common houseplants can pose a threat to your pet's health. Here are some plants that are considered **poisonous** to parrots:

- amaryllis
- calla lily
- daffodil
- dieffenbachia
- English ivy
- foxglove
- holly
- lily-of-the-valley
- mistletoe
- rhubarb

What's a budgie owner to do? Are there any safe plants that you can keep in your home without endangering your feathered friend? Fortunately, yes, there are.

Some plants that are considered **safe** for bird owners to have in their homes include:

- African violets
- aloe
- burro's tail
- Christmas cactus
- edible fig
- ferns
- gardenia
- grape ivy

action on your part to help save your bird from serious injury or death. I'd like to outline some basic first aid techniques that may prove useful in these situations.

Before we get into the specific techniques, make sure you have your bird owner's first aid kit (see sidebar in this chapter for information on what to include).

In *The Complete Bird Owner's Handbook*, veterinarian Gary Gallerstein offers the following advice to bird owners whose birds need urgent care:

No matter what the situation, there are a few things to keep in mind when facing a medical emergency with your pet. First, keep as calm as possible because your bird is already excited enough from being injured, and your getting excited won't help your pet get well. Next, stop any bleeding, keep the bird warm and minimize handling it.

After you've stabilized your pet, call your veterinarian's office for further instructions. Tell them "This is an emergency" and that your bird has had an accident. Describe what happened to your pet as clearly and calmly as you can. Listen carefully to the instructions you are given and follow them. Finally, transport your bird to the vet's office as quickly and safely as you can.

Here are some urgent medical situations that bird owners are likely to encounter, the reason that they are medical emergencies, the signs and symptoms your bird might show and the recommended treatments for the problem.

ANIMAL BITES

Infections can develop from bacteria on the biting animal's teeth and/or claws. Also, a bird's internal organs can be damaged by the bite. Sometimes the bite marks can be seen, but often the bird shows few, if any, signs of injury.

Call your veterinarian's office and transport the bird there immediately. Treatment for shock and antibiotics are often the course of action veterinarians take to save birds that have been bitten.

BEAK INJURY

A bird needs both its upper and lower beak (also called the upper and lower mandible) to eat and preen properly. Infections can also set in rather quickly if a beak is fractured or punctured.

An obvious symptom is the bird is bleeding from its beak. This often occurs after the bird flies into a windowpane or mirror, or if it has a run-in with an operational ceiling fan. The beak may also be cracked or damaged in which case portions of the beak may be missing.

Control bleeding. Keep bird calm and quiet. Contact your avian veterinarian's office.

BLEEDING

A bird can only withstand about a 20 percent loss of blood volume (in a budgie, about twelve drops) and still recover from an injury. In the event of external bleeding, you will see blood on the bird, its cage and its surroundings. In the case of internal bleeding, the bird may pass bloody droppings or bleed from its nose, mouth or vent.

For external bleeding, apply direct pressure. If the bleeding doesn't stop with direct pressure, apply a coagulant, such as styptic powder (for nails and beaks) or cornstarch (for broken feathers and skin injuries). If the bleeding stops, observe the bird to make sure the bleeding does not resume and the bird

FIRST AID KIT

I suggest that you assemble a bird owner's first aid kit so that you will have some basic supplies on hand before your bird needs them. Here's what to include:

- appropriate-sized towels for catching and holding your bird

- a heating pad, heat lamp or other heat source

- styptic powder or cornstarch to stop bleeding (use styptic powder on beak and nails only)

- blunt-tipped scissors

- nail clippers and nail file

- needle-nosed pliers to pull broken blood feathers

- blunt-end tweezers

- hydrogen peroxide or other disinfectant solution

- eye irrigation solution

- bandage materials such as gauze squares, masking tape (it doesn't stick to a bird's feathers like adhesive tape does) and gauze rolls

- Pedialyte or other energy supplement

- eye dropper

- penlight

does not go into shock. Call your veterinarian's office if the bird seems weak or if it has lost a lot of blood and arrange to take the bird in for further treatment.

In the case of broken blood feathers, you may have to remove the feather shaft to stop the bleeding. To do this, grasp the feather shaft as close to the skin as you can with a pair of needle-nosed pliers and pull out the shaft with a swift, steady motion. Apply direct pressure to the skin after you remove the feather shaft.

BREATHING PROBLEMS

Respiratory problems in pet birds can be life threatening. The bird wheezes or clicks while breathing, bobs its tail, breathes with an open mouth, and has discharge from its nares or swelling around its eyes.

Keep the bird warm, place it in a bathroom with a hot shower running to help it breathe easier and call your veterinarian's office.

BURNS

Birds that are burned severely enough can go into shock and may die. A burned bird has reddened skin and burnt or greasy feathers. The bird may also show signs of shock (see below for details).

Mist the burned area with cool water. Apply antibiotic cream or spray lightly. **Do not apply any oily or greasy substances,** including butter. If the bird seems shocky or the burn is widespread, contact your veterinarian's office immediately for further instructions.

CONCUSSION

A concussion results from a sharp blow to the head that can cause injury to the brain. Birds sometimes suffer concussions when they fly into mirrors or windows. They will seem stunned and may go into shock.

Keep the bird warm, prevent it from hurting itself further and watch it carefully. Alert your veterinarian's office to the injury.

Cloacal Prolapse

In this situation the bird's lower intestines, uterus or cloaca is protruding from its vent. You will notice pink, red, brown or black tissue protruding from its vent.

Contact your veterinarian's office for immediate follow-up care. Your veterinarian can usually reposition the organs.

Egg Binding

The egg blocks the hen's excretory system and makes it impossible for her to eliminate. Also, eggs can sometimes break inside the hen, which can lead to infection. An egg-bound hen strains to lay an egg unsuccessfully. She becomes fluffed and lethargic, sits on the floor of her cage, may be paralyzed and may have a swollen abdomen.

Keep her warm because this sometimes helps her pass the egg. Put her and her cage into a warm bathroom with a hot shower running to increase the humidity, which may also help her pass the egg. If your bird doesn't improve shortly (within a hour), contact your veterinarian.

Eye Injury

Untreated eye problems may lead to blindness. Symptoms include swollen or pasty eyelids, discharge, cloudy eyeball, increased rubbing of eye area.

Examine the eye carefully for foreign bodies. Contact your veterinarian for more information.

Fractures

A fracture can cause a bird to go into shock. Depending on the type of fracture, infections can also set in. Birds most often break bones in their legs, so be on the lookout for a bird that is holding one leg at an odd angle or that isn't putting weight on one leg. Sudden swelling of a leg or wing or a droopy wing can also indicate fractures.

Confine the bird to its cage or a small carrier. Don't handle it unnecessarily. Keep it warm and contact your veterinarian.

FROSTBITE

A bird could lose toes or feet to frostbite. It could also go into shock and die as a result. You will be able to notice that the frostbitten area is very cold and dry to the touch and is pale in color.

Warm up the damaged tissue gradually in a circulating water bath. Keep the bird warm and contact your veterinarian's office for further instructions.

Stained glass can be dangerous to your budgie because of the lead content.

INHALED OR EATEN FOREIGN OBJECT

Birds can develop serious respiratory or digestive problems from foreign objects in their bodies. In the case of inhaled items, symptoms include wheezing and other respiratory problems. In the case of consumed objects, the bird was seen playing with a small item that suddenly cannot be found.

Steps to take: If you suspect that your bird has inhaled or eaten something it shouldn't, contact your veterinarian's office immediately.

LEAD POISONING

Birds can die from lead poisoning. A bird with lead poisoning may act depressed or weak. It may be blind, or it may walk in circles at the bottom of its cage. It may regurgitate or pass droppings that resemble tomato juice.

Contact your avian veterinarian immediately. Lead poisoning requires a quick start to treatment, and the treatment may require several days or weeks to complete successfully.

Note: Lead poisoning is easily prevented by keeping birds away from common sources of lead in the home. These include stained glass items, leaded paint found in some older homes, fishing weights, drapery weights, parrot toys (some are weighted with lead). One item that won't cause lead poisoning is a lead pencil (they're actually graphite).

OVERHEATING

High body temperatures can kill a bird. An overheated bird will try to make itself thin. It will hold its wings away from its body, open its mouth and roll its tongue in an attempt to cool itself. Birds don't have sweat glands, so they must try to cool their bodies by exposing as much of their skin's surface as they can to moving air. Cool the bird off by putting it in front of a fan (make sure the blades are screened so the bird doesn't injure itself further), by spraying it with cool water or by having it stand in a bowl of cool water. Let the bird drink cool water if it can (if it can't, offer it cool water with an eyedropper) and contact your veterinarian.

POISONING

Poisons can kill a small bird quickly. Poisoned birds may suddenly regurgitate, have diarrhea or bloody droppings, and have redness or burns around their mouths. They may also go into convulsions, become paralyzed or go into shock. Put the poison out of your bird's reach. Contact your veterinarian for further instructions. Be prepared to take the poison with you to the vet's office in case he or she needs to contact a poison control center for further information.

Seizures

Seizures can indicate a number of serious conditions, including lead poisoning, infections, nutritional deficiency, heat stroke and epilepsy. The bird goes into a seizure that lasts from a few seconds to a minute. Afterward, it seems dazed and may stay on the cage floor for several hours. It may also appear unsteady and not perch.

Keep the bird from hurting itself further by removing everything you can from its cage. Cover the bird's cage with a towel and darken the room to reduce the bird's stress level. Contact your veterinarian's office for further instructions immediately.

Shock

Shock indicates that the bird's circulatory system cannot move the blood supply around the bird's body. This is a serious condition that can lead to death if left untreated. Shocky birds may act depressed, they may breathe rapidly and they may have a fluffed appearance. If your bird displays these signs in conjunction with a recent accident, suspect shock and take appropriate action.

Keep your bird warm, cover its cage and transport it to your veterinarian's office as soon as possible.

Emergency Tips

Veterinarian Michael Murray recommends that bird owners keep the following tips in mind when facing emergency situations:

> *Keep the bird warm.* You can do this by putting the bird in an empty aquarium with a heating pad under it, by putting a heat lamp near the bird's cage or by putting a heating pad set on low under the bird's cage in place of the cage tray. Whatever heat source you choose to use, make sure to keep a close eye on your bird so that it doesn't accidentally burn itself on the pad or lamp or that it doesn't chew on a power cord.

Put the bird in a dark, quiet room. This helps reduce
the bird's stress.

Put the bird's food in locations that are easy to reach.
Sick birds need to eat, but they may not be able to
reach food in its normal locations in the cage.
Sometimes birds require hand-feeding to keep
their calorie consumption steady.

Protect the bird from additional injury. If the convalesc-
ing bird is in a clear-sided aquarium, for example,
you may want to put a towel over the glass to keep
the bird from flying into it.

Caring for Older Birds

Older pet birds are prone to a number of health problems, including tumors, vision problems, thyroid gland
insufficiencies, chlamydiosis and upper respiratory
infections.

TUMORS

Budgies can develop tumors as early as age five, although
if a bird passes the age of seven without developing a
tumor, it will probably live out its life tumor free. If you
notice that your pet's breastbone sticks out a little more
than it used to or that your bird has difficulty perching, schedule an evaluation with your avian veterinarian;
both of these signs indicate possible tumor development. Tumors develop in pet birds most frequently in
the nerves off the bird's spine. A tumor in this spot can
impair kidney and gonad function, which can put pressure on the nerve that runs into the bird's leg.

VISION PROBLEMS

Vision problems can show themselves in several ways.
Your pet may no longer be able to judge distances well,
or its eyes may appear clouded over. Just as in older
people, cataracts can appear in older budgies.

THYROID PROBLEMS

Thyroid problems occur frequently in older parrots,
but they aren't discussed often. These problems occur

in two main areas: a deficiency in the bird's hormonal system or a need for supplemental iodine in the diet. If your budgie suddenly gains weight and develops fat deposits that resemble tumors, contact your avian veterinarian to have your pet examined.

Although they may not seem to be connected, a thyroid problem may show itself in a longer-than-average molt. If you notice that your budgie's molting period seems unusually long as it ages, talk to your avian veterinarian. A hormonal supplement may be in order to help keep your bird healthy.

Although older budgies are far from being delicate "hothouse flowers," owners of these birds should pay more attention to their pets' diets to ensure that the bird continues to receive a varied diet that is low in fat and to the temperature of the room in which the bird is kept during cool weather. Add supplemental heat by using an incandescent bulb covered with a reflector on one end of your bird's cage. This allows a bird to move closer to the heat source if it is cold and away from it if the bird becomes too warm. Make sure that the bulb is far enough away from the cage so that your pet cannot burn itself on the reflector or the bulb.

As your budgie ages, the need to watch its daily routine becomes even more important, since health problems that are caught early are easier to treat.

When Your Budgie Dies

Although birds are relatively long-lived pets, eventually the wonderful relationship between bird and owner ends when the bird dies. While no one has an easy time accepting the death of a beloved pet, children may have more difficulty with the loss than adults.

Let your child know that it's okay to feel sad about losing your budgie. Encourage your child to draw pictures of the bird, to make a collage using photos of your pet budgie or pictures of budgies from magazines, to write stories or poems about it or to talk about your loss. Also explain to the child that these sad feelings will pass with time.

Regardless of a child's age, being honest about the loss of your budgie is the best approach to help all family members cope with the loss.

While helping their children cope with the death of a pet, parents need to remember that it's okay for adults to feel sad, too. Don't diminish your feelings of loss by saying "It's only a bird." Pets fill important roles in our lives and our families. Whenever we lose someone close to us, we grieve. If someone in your family needs to discuss the loss further, the University of California has established a pet loss support hot line. Call 916/752-4200 for further information. The Delta Society also maintains a directory of pet loss resources. More information about this directory is available by calling 206/226-7357. Your avian veterinarian's office may know of pet loss support groups in your area, or you may be able

to find one by contacting a local animal shelter or SPCA office. Finally, some pet loss support groups are available online through the Internet.

Always remember the good times you've had with your budgie.

Although you may feel as though you never want another bird because of the pain caused by your budgie's death, don't let the loss of your budgie keep you from owning other birds. While you can never replace your budgie completely, you may find that you miss having a feathered companion around your house. Some people will want a new pet bird almost immediately after suffering a loss, while others will want to wait a few weeks or months before bringing another bird home. Maybe you want another budgie, or perhaps you'd like to try owning a different avian species. Discuss bringing home a new pet bird with your family, your avian veterinarian and bird breeders in your area. Together, I'm sure you can work out a plan that's best for you!

Enjoying

Your

part three

Budgie

chapter 8

Budgie
Behavior

Common Budgie Behaviors

The following common budgerigar behaviors are listed in alphabetical order to help you better understand your new feathered friend!

BEAK GRINDING

If you hear your bird making odd little grinding noises as it's drifting off to sleep, don't be alarmed! Beak grinding is a sign of a contented budgie, and it's commonly heard as a bird settles in for the night.

BEAK WIPING

After a meal, it's common for a budgie to wipe its beak against a perch or on the cage floor to clean it. If something particularly persistent is stuck to a budgie's beak, it will use its foot to clean its beak.

BIRDIE AEROBICS

This is how I describe a sudden bout of stretching that all parrots seem prone to. An otherwise calm bird will suddenly grab the cage bars and stretch the wing and leg muscles on one side of its body, or it will raise both wings high.

EYE PINNING

This is what happens when your budgie sees something that excites it. Its pupils will be large, then contract, then go large again. Birds will pin their eyes when they see a favorite food, a favored person, another bird or a special toy. In larger parrots, this can also be a sign of confused emotions that can leave an owner vulnerable to a nasty bite. Your budgie may also bite when it's in "emotional overload," so watch out!

FEATHER PICKING

Don't confuse this with preening (see below). Feather picking

Mutual preening is an honor the budgie reserves for its favorite companions. If your budgie tries to preen you, consider it a sign of great affection!

results from physiological problems, such as a dietary imbalance, a hormonal change, a thyroid problem or a infection of the skin or feathers. It can also be caused by an emotional upset, such as a change in the owner's appearance, a change in the bird's routine, another pet being added to the home, a new baby in the home or a number of other factors. Once feather picking begins, it may be difficult to get a bird to stop. Although it looks painful to us, some birds find

103

the routine of pulling out their feathers emotionally soothing. The good news is that budgies are not as prone to this condition as other larger parrots are. If you keep more than one budgie, however, be aware that they sometimes pick out each other's feathers. If this occurs, you may have to house your birds in separate cages to allow the plucked bird to regrow its plumage.

Your budgie preens to keep its feathers healthy and clean.

FLUFFING

This is often a prelude to preening or a tension releaser. If your bird fluffs up, stays fluffed and resembles a little feathered pinecone, however, contact your avian veterinarian for an appointment because fluffed feathers can be an indicator of illness.

JEALOUSY

Some budgies become very possessive of their owners, and these jealous birds demonstrate their displeasure in a number of ways. These can include tearing up their cages, nibbling on their owners' hands or screaming that, while not as annoying as the noise made by a cockatoo or macaw, can nonetheless diminish your enjoyment of your budgie as a pet. To prevent your budgie from becoming a problem pet, be sure to provide it the opportunity to entertain itself in its cage alone from time to time. Don't reward its screaming for attention (you'll soon learn which screams are just for the joy of making noise and which ones indicate a pet in danger or pain), and don't bribe your pet into silence with treats while you are out of the room or on the phone. If you do, your bird will soon have you wrapped around its wing feathers and will take full advantage of the situation.

Mutual Preening

This is part of the preening behavior described below, and it can take place between birds or between birds and their owners. It is a sign of affection reserved for best friends or mates, so consider it an honor if your budgie wants to preen your eyebrows, hair, mustache or beard, or your arms and hands.

Pair Bonding

Not only mated pairs bond, but best bird buddies of the same sex will demonstrate some of the same behavior, including sitting close to each other, preening each other and mimicking the other's actions, such as stretching or scratching, often at the same time.

Preening

This is part of a budgie's normal routine. You will see your bird ruffling and straightening its feathers each day. It will also take oil from the uropygial or preen gland at the base of its tail and put the oil on the rest of its feathers, so don't be concerned if you see your pet seeming to peck or bite at its tail. If, during molting, your bird seems to remove

---

FEATHERED WARNINGS

Your bird's feathers are one of the most fascinating organs of its body. The bird uses feathers for movement, warmth and balance, among other things. The following are some feather-related behaviors that can indicate health problems for your budgie.

Fluffing: A healthy budgie will fluff before preening or for short periods. If your budgie seems to remain fluffed up for an extended period, see your avian veterinarian. This can be a sign of illness in birds.

Mutual preening: Two birds will preen each other affectionately, but if you notice excessive feather loss, make sure one bird is not picking on the other and pulling out healthy feathers.

Feather picking: A healthy bird will preen often to keep its feathers in top shape. However, a bird under stress may start to preen excessively and severe feather loss can result.

whole feathers, don't panic! Old, worn feathers are pushed out by incoming new ones, which makes the old feathers loose and easy to remove.

REGURGITATING

If you see that your bird is pinning its eyes, bobbing its head and pumping its neck and crop muscles, it is about to regurgitate some food for you. Birds regurgitate to their mates during breeding season and to their young while raising chicks. It is a mark of great affection to have your bird regurgitate its dinner for you, so try not to be too disgusted if your pet starts bringing up its last meal for you.

Your budgie's vocalizations are good indicators of its mental state.

RESTING ON ONE FOOT

Do not be alarmed if you see your budgie occasionally resting on only one foot. This is normal behavior (the resting foot is often drawn up into the belly feathers). If you see your bird always using both feet to perch, please contact your avian veterinarian because this can indicate a health problem.

SIDE-STEPPING

This is a common movement when a budgie is working its way across its cage on a perch. Other common movements include climbing and flying (if the cage is large enough).

SCRATCHING

Budgies have remarkably flexible leg joints, which they sometimes use to bring their legs up and behind their wings to scratch their heads. Budgies may be the only psittacine birds that do this; larger parrots bring their heads and feet together in front of their bodies to scratch.

STRESS

This can show itself in many ways in your bird's behavior, including shaking, diarrhea, rapid breathing, wing and tail fanning, screaming, feather picking, poor sleeping habits or loss of appetite. Over a period of time, stress can harm your budgie's health. To prevent your bird from becoming stressed, try to provide it with as normal and regular a routine as possible. Parrots are, for the most part, creatures of habit, and they don't always adapt well to sudden changes in their environment or schedule. But if you do have to change something, talk to your parrot about it first. I know it seems crazy, but telling your bird what you're going to do before you do it may actually help reduce its stress. I received this advice from avian behaviorist Christine Davis, and now I explain what I'm doing every time I rearrange the living room or leave him at the vet's office for boarding during business trips. If you're going to be away on vacation, tell your bird how long you'll be gone, and count the days out on your fingers in front of the bird or show it a calendar.

VOCALIZATION

Many parrots vocalize around sunrise and sunset, which I believe hearkens back to flock behavior in the wild when wild parrots call to each other to start and end their days. Budgies are no exceptions to this rule, especially at day's end when they chirp softly as they ready themselves for sleep. You may also notice if you keep more than one budgie that the birds will call to each other during the day if they are in separate rooms (perhaps one is on a playgym in the family room while the other is in its cage in the dining room). These contact calls help birds keep track of each other, both in the wild and in your home. If something startles your budgie, you may hear it make a short, shrill call to signal that something has alarmed it. Budgies can also express their pleasure or displeasure through vocalization. Soft chirps indicate a happy bird, while shrieks indicate that something is amiss in your bird's world.

Taming Your Budgie

Taming a parrot was one of the most popular topics of discussion when I worked at *Bird Talk*, and the discussion continues today between avian behaviorists and their clients in bird club meetings, books and magazine articles, and on the Internet.

"Time out" in a covered cage can help calm down excited birds.

Training a budgie (or any bird) takes a great deal of time and patience on the part of the bird owner. You must first gain your pet's trust, and then you must work

to never lose it. To maintain this, you must be careful not to lose your temper with your bird and *never* hit it. Birds are very sensitive, intelligent creatures that do not deserve to be hit, no matter how you may feel in a moment of anger.

Although parrots are clever creatures, they are not linear "cause and effect" thinkers. If a parrot commits action A (chewing on some molding under your kitchen cabinets, for example), it won't associate reaction B (you yelling at it, locking it in its cage or otherwise punishing it) with the original misbehavior. As a result, most traditional forms of discipline are ineffective with parrots.

So what do you do when your budgie misbehaves? Try to catch it in the act. Look at it sternly (what bird behaviorist Sally Blanchard calls "the evil eye") and tell it "No" in a firm voice. If the bird is climbing on or chewing something it shouldn't, also remove it from the source of danger and temptation as you tell it "No." If your bird has wound itself up into a screaming banshee, sometimes a little "time out" in its cage (between five and ten minutes in most cases) with the cover on does wonders to calm it down. Once the screaming stops and the bird calms down enough to play quietly, eat or simply move around its cage, the cover comes off to reveal a well-behaved, calmed-down pet.

"Time out" in a covered cage can help calm down excited birds. A good first step in taming your budgie is getting it to become comfortable around you. To do this, give your bird a bit of warning before you approach its cage. Don't sneak up on your bird, and try not to startle it. Call its name when you walk into the room. Try to be quiet and to move slowly around your pet because these gestures will help it become more comfortable with you. Keep your hands behind you, and reassure the bird that you aren't there to harm it, that everything is all right and that it's a wonderful pet.

After your bird is comfortable having you in the same room with it, you may want to try placing your hand in its cage as a first step toward taking it out of its cage. Place your hand in your bird's cage and hold it there for a few seconds. Don't be surprised if your bird flutters around and squawks at first at the "intruder."

Continue this process daily, and leave your hand in the cage for slightly longer periods of time each day. Within a few days, your budgie won't make a fuss about your hand being in its space, and it may come over to investigate this new perch. Do not remove your hand from the bird cage the first time your budgie lands on it; just let the bird become accustomed to perching on your hand.

After several successful perching attempts on successive days, try to take your hand out of the cage with your bird on it. Some budgies will take to this new adventure willingly, while others are reluctant to leave the safety and security of home. (Be sure your bird's wings are clipped and all doors and windows are secured before taking your bird out of its cage.)

If your bird doesn't seem to respond to this method, you can try an alternate taming method. Take the bird out of its cage and into a small room, such as a bathroom, that has been bird-proofed (i.e., the toilet lid is down, the shower door is closed and the bathroom hasn't been cleaned with any cleansers with strong chemical odors recently). Sit down on the floor, place your bird in front of you and begin playing with the bird. Don't be surprised if your bird tries to fly a few times. With clipped wings, however, it won't get very far and will give up trying after a few failed attempts.

Calm your budgie by holding it on your chest where it can hear your heartbeat.

Breeder Charlene Beane has demonstrated her budgie taming method for me several times, and its simplicity and effectiveness always amazes me. Charlene will hold a bird that isn't quite tame close to her chest so the bird can hear her heartbeat, which seems to calm the bird. She then talks to it in a low, soothing tone and explains to it that it will make someone a wonderful pet. As she does this, she gently begins to stroke the budgie's back, which helps the bird to relax. She continues to explain its role as a perfect pet for about five minutes, stroking it as she talks. Pretty soon, the bird is calm and ready to be handled.

Once you've calmed your budgie using Charlene's method, see if you can make perching on your hand a game for your pet. Once it masters perching on your hand, you can teach it to step up by gently pressing your finger up and into the bird's belly. This will cause the bird to step up. As it does so, say "Step up" or "Up."

Before long, your bird will respond to this command without much prompting.

Along with the "Up" command, you may want to teach your budgie the "Down" command. When you put the bird down on its cage or playgym, simply say "Down" as the bird steps off your hand. These two simple commands offer a great deal of control for you over your bird, because you can say "Up" to put an unruly bird back in its cage or you can tell a parrot that needs to go to bed "Down" as you put the bird in its cage at night.

After your bird has mastered the "Up" and "Down" commands, encourage it to climb a "ladder" by moving it from index finger to index finger (the "rungs"). Keep taming sessions short (about ten minutes is the maximum budgie attention span) and make the taming process fun because it will be much more enjoyable for both of you.

To teach your budgie the "Up" command, hold a finger to its abdomen while it is perching on your finger.

After your pet has become comfortable sitting on your hand, try petting it. Birds seem to like to have their heads, backs, cheek patches, under wing areas and eye areas (including the closed eyelids) scratched or petted lightly. Quite a few like to have a spot low on their backs at the bases of their tails (over their preen glands) rubbed. Many birds do not enjoy having their stomachs scratched, although yours may think this is heaven! You'll have to experiment to see where your bird likes to be petted. You'll know you're successful if your bird clicks or grinds its beak, pins its eyes or settles onto your hand or into your

Teach your budgie the "Up" command by holding a finger to its abdomen while it is perching on your finger.

111

lap with a completely relaxed, blissful expression on its face.

Some people may try to tell you that you need to wear gloves while taming your budgie. I'd recommend against this for two reasons: First, a budgie generally doesn't bite *that* hard, and wearing gloves will only make your hands appear more scary to your bird. If your pet is scared, taming it will take more time and patience on your part, which may make the process less enjoyable for you.

Toilet Training

Although some people don't believe it, budgies and other parrots can be toilet trained so they don't defecate on their owners. If you want to toilet train your bird, you will have to choose a word that will indicate the act of defecating to your pet, such as "Go poop" or "Go potty." While you're training your pet to associate the chosen phrase with the action, you will have to train yourself to your budgie's body language and actions that indicate it is about to defecate, such as shifting around or squatting slightly.

Once your bird seems to associate "Go potty" with defecating, you can try picking it up and holding it until it starts to shift or squat. Tell the bird to "Go potty" while placing it on its cage, where it can defecate. Once it's done, pick it up again and praise it for being such a smart bird! Expect a few accidents while you are both learning this trick, and soon you'll have a toilet-trained bird that you can put on its cage about every twenty minutes or so, give it the command and expect the bird to defecate on command.

Will My Budgie Talk?

One of the most appealing aspects of budgie ownership is this species' reputation as talented talkers. Although many budgies learn to talk, none of them is guaranteed to talk. The tips offered below will help you teach your budgie to talk, but please don't be disappointed if your pet never utters a word.

Remember that language, whether it's budgie or human, helps members of a species or group communicate. Most baby birds learn the language of their parents because it helps them communicate within their family and their flock. A pet budgie raised with people may learn to imitate the sounds it hears its human family make, but if you have more than one budgie, the birds may find communicating with each other easier and seemingly more enjoyable than trying to learn your language.

Although most budgies raised around humans do learn to talk, some choose to make other sounds. Calvin, the physically challenged bird I used to bird-sit, had ample opportunity to learn human speech from his owner and other people who saw him regularly. Instead of speaking, though, Calvin chose to imitate the computer printer, modem and other machines found in his owner's office!

> ### DR. IRENE PEPPERBERG AND ALEX
>
> An African Grey named Alex, who is being studied by Irene M. Pepperberg, PhD, at the University of Arizona, has a 100-word vocabulary, can count to six and correctly answer questions about the size, shape, color and number of objects shown him. He can categorize objects, telling a questioner what traits the objects have in common or how they differ. Not bad for a "birdbrain"!

According to budgie breeder Penny Corbett, the best time to teach a budgie to talk is between the time it leaves the nest and its first birthday. If you have an adult budgie, the chances of it learning to talk are less than if you start with a young bird. Male birds may be more likely to talk, but I have heard of some talkative females, too.

TALKING TRAINING TIPS

You will be more successful in training a budgie to talk if you keep a single pet bird, rather than a pair. Birds kept in pairs or groups are more likely to bond with other birds than to want to bond with people. By the same token, don't give your bird any toys with mirrors on them if you want the bird to learn to talk, since your bird will think that the bird in the mirror is a potential cagemate with whom it can bond.

Start with a young bird because the younger the bird is, the more likely it is to want to mimic human speech.

Pick one phrase to start with. Keep it short and simple, such as the bird's name. Say the phrase slowly so that the bird learns it clearly. Some people teach their budgies to talk by rattling off words and phrases quickly, only to be disappointed when the bird repeats them in a blurred jumble that cannot be understood.

Be sure to say the chosen phrase with emphasis and enthusiasm. Birds like a "drama reward" and seem to learn words that are said emphatically, which may be why some of them pick up bad language so quickly!

Try to have phrases make sense. For instance, say "Good morning" or "Hello" when you uncover the bird's cage each day. Say "Good-bye" when you leave the room, or ask "Want a treat?" when you offer your budgie its meals. (Phrases that make sense are also more likely to be used by you and other members of your family when conversing with your bird. The more your bird hears an interesting word or phrase, the more likely it is to say that phrase some day.)

If you are hoping to get your budgie to talk, avoid mirror toys. Your bird may bond with the budgie in the mirror rather than with you.

Don't change the phrase around. If you're teaching your bird to say "Hello," for example, don't say "Hello" one day, then "Hi" the next, followed by "Hi Petey!" (or whatever your bird's name is) another day.

Keep training sessions short. Budgie breeders recommend ten- to fifteen-minute sessions.

Train your bird in a quiet area. Think of how distracting it is when someone is trying to talk to you with a radio or television blaring in the background. It's hard to hear what the other person is saying under those conditions, isn't it? Your budgie won't be able to hear you any better or understand what you are trying to accomplish if you try to train it in the midst of noisy distractions. Be sure to keep your budgie involved in your family's routine, though, because isolating it completely won't help it feel comfortable and part of the family. Remember that a bird needs to feel comfortable in its environment before it will draw attention to itself by talking.

Be patient with your pet. Stop the sessions if you find you are getting frustrated. Your budgie will sense that something is bothering you and will react by becoming bothered itself. This is not an ideal situation for you or your bird. Try to keep your mood upbeat. Smile a lot and praise your pet when it does well!

Graduate to more difficult phrases as your bird masters simple words. Consider keeping a log of the words your bird knows (this is especially helpful if more than one person will be working with the budgie).

When you aren't talking to your budgie, try listening to it. Budgies and other birds sometimes mumble to themselves to practice talking as they drift off to sleep. Because a budgie has a very small voice, you'll have to listen carefully to hear if your pet is making progress.

You're probably wondering if the talking tapes and compact discs sold in pet stores and through advertisements in bird magazines work. The most realistic answer I can give is "sometimes." Some birds learn from the repetition of the tapes and CDs that, fortunately, have gotten livelier and more interesting in recent years. Other birds benefit from having their owners make tapes of the phrases the bird is currently learning and hearing those tapes play when their owners aren't around. I would recommend against a constant barrage of taped phrases during the day, because the bird is likely to get bored hearing the same thing for hours on end. If it's bored, the bird will be more likely to tune out the tape and the training in the process.

Finally, if your patient, consistent training seems to be going nowhere, you may have to accept the fact that your budgie isn't going to talk. We finally had to do this with my budgie, Charlie. Despite my mother's most patient attempts to teach the bird to say "Pretty bird," he never learned to talk. My mother did things by the book, too. She spoke in a bright, cheerful voice, she kept the training sessions short, she kept a positive attitude and tone when talking to the bird, and she displayed patience that rivaled Job's, but Charlie remained silent. Perhaps he was too old, perhaps he was too isolated, or perhaps he just wasn't interested in the phrase.

As I've said before, don't be too disappointed if your pet doesn't learn to talk. As one *Bird Talk* reader explained it, "talking should be the icing on the cake," rather than the primary reason for owning a bird. If you end up with a nontalking pet, continue to love it for the unique creature that it is, rather than what you want it to be.

TALKING SUCCESS STORIES

Although budgies aren't guaranteed to talk, Puck, a budgie in northern California, holds the Guinness World Record for largest vocabulary of any animal. Puck's owner estimates that her bird has a 1,728-word vocabulary!

Sparkie, a budgie that lived in Great Britain from 1954 to 1962, held the record for a talking bird in his time. He won the BBC's Cage Word Contest in 1958 by reciting eight four-line nursery rhymes without stopping. At the time of his death, Sparkie had a vocabulary of 531 words and 383 sentences.

chapter 9

Your **Beautiful** Budgie

Budgie Showing

You've really come to enjoy your pet budgie and other budgie owners you've met through visits to your favorite bird supply store and your avian veterinarian's office. You want to take the next step—showing your bird—but you're unsure of how to go about it.

JOINING A BIRD CLUB

First, you need to join a bird club. Attend meetings of your local bird club to see if they have exhibitors who are willing to help people new to showing birds (like you). Go to bird shows as an observer and see which birds win. Talk to the breeders of those birds after the show to see if they have chicks available that you can purchase. Ask the breeder of your birds, as well as other breeders in the club, to help you start training your birds for the show season, which kicks into high gear in the fall.

Once you have some promising show birds, you'll need to know when the show is happening. Bird magazines, club newsletters and even bulletin boards in pet stores and veterinary offices can be good places to locate this information. Along with the date and location of the event, a contact person's name, address and phone number are usually listed. Call or write this person to obtain a show catalog, which is your guide to the particulars of the show you've chosen to enter. When you make your catalog request, ask again for the date and location of the show, along with the name of the hotel most of the exhibitors will be staying in (this is especially important if you will be traveling to the show, since you'll probably want to make some new friends along the way).

As you read over the show catalog, note the check-in time for your birds (late birds don't have to be accepted for judging) and any entry fees. You will also learn who will be judging your category and what time judging is set to begin, along with what awards will be given out.

The show catalog will also contain information on the divisions, subdivisions, sections and classes that will be judged in this show. Study this information carefully, because you will need to know what information to write down on your show tags and entry forms. Birds that are entered in the wrong classification may be disqualified, so make sure the information you put on your forms is correct.

As you fill out your forms, you will have to decide what level of competition you want to enter: novice, intermediate or champion. You can enter at either novice or intermediate, but you cannot drop back to novice if you choose intermediate. (Budgie fanciers between the ages of seven and seventeen may be able to enter an ABS show in the junior division, but not all shows include this division.)

A novice or an intermediate becomes a champion when the exhibitor places a bird on the top bench in its division and/or places a bird in the Top Ten of the show.

What are the Judges Looking For?

The show catalog will also contain the judging standard for the birds that will be shown. Most budgie shows use the American Budgerigar Society standard, which is the standard of perfection for the ideal budgerigar. So far, this ideal bird does not yet exist, but breeders keep trying.

The ideal male bird is described by the American Budgerigar Society as having "a round and full crown (hens may have lower domes), a good rise and a wide and bold frontal [forehead]; a clean and neat cere; a well-tucked-in beak; a low and wide mask that is well-placed and has large round spots; a full-shouldered front line that gradually tapers to the tail; strong legs and feet that grip the perch firmly; a straight tail held in line with the body and with a length that is in proper proportion to the body; flight feathers that are whipped together, not crossed; wings that are held neatly in line with the body; an almost straight back line that is not hollow or hoopy; full, wide shoulders with no appearance of a neckline; a correctly located and bright eye; and a full back skull that has sufficient distance to the eye."

In the wild, the budgie's color is green, but in captivity many amazing color combinations have been established.

Budgie breeder and judge Penny J. Corbett described the criteria a judge uses to evaluate budgies this way in *Bird Talk:* "The bird must be in good condition. This applies to cleanliness, health, physical condition and full plumage. . . . The head should be large, wide, round and symmetrical. The neck should be short and wide and join to the body smoothly. The body should gracefully taper from the neck nape to the tail. There should be a straight back line. The chest should be neither excessively full nor shallow, and the body should be in proportion. The tail should have both long tail feathers and should be straight and tight following the natural continuation of the body line. Legs and feet should be straight and strong with no toes missing. The wings are to be neatly shaped and should not cross. The eyes are to be bright and positioned well. A small beak is to be neatly set well into the face. The cere must be clean and in proportion to the beak size. The color and texture must be appropriate to sex and variety."

Corbett continues, "A bird that is steady on the perch with an alert and natural look makes up the position and training of the bird. Even the nicest bird will not have a

If your show bird develops pinfeathers shortly before the show, you will want to reconsider entering it.

chance to wing if it was not trained to 'show.' The 'ideal' budgie is approximately nine inches long. The size of nine inches is for an equally proportioned bird. The bird's color is to be of an even shade that is clear and distinct. The deep, clear, wide mask is ornamented by four evenly spaced spots, supported by two spots under the cheek patches, a total of six spots. These six spots are, again, to be in proportion to the birds. All of the markings are to be well balanced and neat."

LOOKING GOOD

Now that you have an idea of what the judges are looking for, how do you get your budgie to live up to its own standard of perfection? You train it and groom it and show it off in a proper show cage.

Show birds must demonstrate grace under pressure during judging. They must appear calm, but alert, and comfortable in their show cages (which may or may not be their regular cages). They must also be able to accept and adjust to a stranger looking closely at them and tapping on their cages. Finally, they must be in perfect feather and tip-top overall condition. Sounds like a tall order? It is, but it can be done!

To train your budgie for the show circuit, get it used to its show cage well before show season starts. You will need to have a clean cage that is in good shape to show your budgie to its best advantage. Again, an experienced exhibitor can help you with this important aspect of showing your bird. Several months before its first show, put your budgie's show cage where your bird can see it. Gradually move the show cage closer to your bird's home. When your bird appears curious about it but not frightened, put your budgie in the show cage with the cage door open. Allow your pet to explore the new cage, but encourage it to stay on its perch.

Your potential show budgie will need to be healthy, alert and patient as well as good-looking.

After your budgie has learned to stay on the perch, invite some friends over to simulate a show. Reinforce your pet's good behavior (staying on its perch and not showing signs of panic) with praise and a small treat after "the show."

Next, ask a friend to "judge" your bird. Have this person get close to the cage and give your budgie a thorough visual inspection. Ask the "judge" to tap lightly on the show cage with a pointer or pencil and to poke gently at the bird with this object. Praise your bird for its good behavior. (If, however, your bird seems

121

uncomfortable with this added attention, you may want to reconsider the show circuit for this bird.)

After you have your bird trained, you'll need to work on its grooming. To show well, it will need to be fully feathered, have its wings and nails trimmed and its feet cleaned. If your bird suddenly breaks out in pinfeathers, you may want to reconsider showing it at that time, or you may want to still enter the show as practice.

One area that judges look at in budgies is the face spots. Ideally, budgies should have six of these spots, but many times one spot runs into another naturally. You may have to help your bird's appearance by pulling the spots that don't belong. Ask a more experienced exhibitor to demonstrate this procedure for you.

After you've polished your bird's show style, it's time to work on your own. Here are some tips offered by Pamela L. Higdon in *Bird Talk* magazine to help make your first experience as a budgie exhibitor an enjoyable one:

- Enter only healthy birds in the show.

- Follow all rules, signs and notices at the show.

- Maintain a positive attitude throughout the show.

- Show consideration for show staff members and fellow exhibitors.

- Remain in designated areas during judging.

- Be a good loser and an even better winner.

- Remember, all judging decisions are final.

THE AMERICAN BUDGERIGAR SOCIETY

If you are serious about showing budgies, you will probably want to join a bird club that is affiliated with the American Budgerigar Society (ABS). This organization of breeders and exhibitors of predominantly English, or exhibition, budgies, was founded in Indianapolis, Indiana, in 1941.

The goal of the ABS is "to encourage the interest of fanciers in budgies as an outstanding exhibition species; to encourage the interest of the general public in budgies as charming and interesting pets; to study the breeding habits of budgies and promote interest in better breeding habits; to study the dietary requirements of budgies and promote interest in better nutrition; to study the diseases of budgies and disseminate information as to the best methods of prevention and cure; and to promote, through the formation of a panel of qualified judges and the adoption of a standard of perfection, the showing of budgies bred to an ideal."

Along with local shows held by member clubs, the ABS hosts an annual All American show where members and their birds can compete against one another. The location for this show is chosen two years in advance of the actual show date, and different ABS clubs bid for the honor of hosting the All American.

American budgies can be shown, too, but they may not be able to be entered in as many shows as their English counterparts. Some shows may have special sections for American budgies, while others may have a whole division for them. Still other shows may have you exhibit your budgie as an Australian parakeet.

part four

Beyond the Basics

chapter 10

For More
Information

For more information on bird care, look for these books at your local library, bookstore or pet store:

Alderton, David, with illustrations by Graeme Stevenson. *Atlas of Parrots of the World*. 1991. TFH Publications Inc.

——— *Birdkeeper's Guide to Budgies*. 1988. Tetra Press.

——— *Birdkeeper's Guide to Parrots and Macaws*. 1989. Tetra Press.

——— *You and Your Pet Bird*. 1994. Alfred A. Knopf.

Birmelin, Immanuel, and Annette Wolter. *The New Parakeet Handbook*. 1986. Barron's Educational Series Inc.

Gallerstein, Gary A. DVM. *The Complete Bird Owner's Handbook*. 1994. Howell Book House.

Magazines

Bird Breeder. Bimonthly magazine dedicated to the concerns of bird breeders who raise and sell pet birds. Subscription information: P.O. Box 420235, Palm Coast, FL 32142-0235.

Bird Talk. Monthly magazine devoted to pet bird ownership. Subscription information: P.O. Box 57347, Boulder, CO 80322-7347.

Birds USA. Annual magazine aimed at first-time bird owners. Look for it in your local bookstore or pet store.

Caged Bird Hobbyist. This magazine for pet bird owners is published seven times a year. Subscription information: 5400 NW 84 Ave., Miami, FL 33166-3333.

Parakeets YearBOOK. Published by yearBOOKS Inc., 1 TFH Plaza, Neptune, NJ 07753. Look for it in your local pet store or bookstore.

Online Resources

Bird-specific sites have been cropping up regularly on the Internet. These sites offer pet bird owners the opportunity to share stories about their pets and trade helpful hints about bird care.

If you belong to an online service, look for the pet site (it's sometimes included in more general topics, such as "Hobbies and Interests," or more specifically "Pets"). If you have Internet access, use your Web browser or WebCrawler to search for "parrots" or "pet birds."

Bird Clubs

The American Budgerigar Society
1704 Kangaroo
Killeen, TX 76543

The American Federation of Aviculture
P.O. Box 56218
Phoenix, AZ 85079-6128

Australian Aviculture
52 Harris Rd.
Elliminyt, Victoria 3249, Australia

Avicultural Society of America
P.O. Box 5516
Riverside, CA 92517-5517

International Avicultural Society
P.O. Box 280383
Memphis, TN 38168

Society of Parrot Breeders and Exhibitors
P.O. Box 369
Groton, MA 01450